Jay Rayner is an ...ning writer, journalist and broadcaster ... collection of shirts. He has written on e... ...g from crime and politics through cinema and th...re to the visual arts, but is best known as the restaurant critic for the *Observer*. For a while he was a sex columnist for *Cosmopolitan*; he also once got himself completely waxed in the name of journalism. He only mentions this because it hurt. Jay is a former Young Journalist of the Year, Critic of the Year and Restaurant Critic of the Year, though not all in the same year. In 2018 he was named Restaurant Writer of the Year in the Fortnum & Mason Food and Drink Awards. Somehow, he has also found time to publish four novels and seven works of non-fiction. He performs live all over the country, both with his own one-man shows and as a pianist with his jazz ensemble, The Jay Rayner Quartet. He is a regular on British television, where he is familiar as a judge on *Masterchef*; he is the chair of BBC Radio 4's food panel show *The Kitchen Cabinet* and presents the *Out to Lunch* podcast. He likes pig.

JAY RAYNER

CHEWING THE FAT

Tasting Notes from a Greedy Life

First published by Guardian Faber in the UK and USA in 2021
Guardian Faber is an imprint of Faber & Faber Ltd,
Bloomsbury House, 74–77 Great Russell Street,
London WC1B 3DA

Guardian is a registered trademark of
Guardian News & Media Ltd,
Kings Place, 90 York Way, London N1 9GU

Typeset by Faber & Faber Ltd
Printed and bound by CPI Group (UK) Ltd, Croydon CR0 4YY

A CIP record for this book
is available from the British Library

ISBN 978-1-7833-5239-5

2 4 6 8 10 9 7 5 3 1

For Sarah, Charlie, Theo and Ben Codrington,
co-conspirators at the table.

Contents

Introduction: Chewing it Over

My father was a not a big eater. 'I'd be happy if I could just take a pill for my lunch,' he once told me, when I was eight or nine years old. I had already concluded that the adult world could be wilfully baffling, but this seemed unnecessarily provocative. It felt like a betrayal. As a child, an unfocused mess of fat-softened limbs and round edges, I knew that food was great. I loved bacon sandwiches on white bread and chocolate eclairs, and lived for evenings when my parents were short on time and dinner was the convenience of Findus Crispy Pancakes filled with delicious if unidentifiable brown matter. There were cheese and onion flavour crisps and Sherbet Dip Dabs. There were many things.

Happily, my mother was not interested in getting her nutrition from a pill. Claire wanted both to feed and be fed. On Saturday lunchtimes, after my parents had done the weekly shop, my mother would fill the kitchen table with cold cuts and cheeses, and plates laid with slippery ribbons of smoked salmon in the brightest shade of orange. There would be dense fish balls, chopped liver topped with crumbled egg and bagels, for we were Jews through food. There was no space in our lives for God, but there was lots of space for lunch. It was a meal called Fick and Porridge, an adapted Spoonerism of Pick and Forage. It was one of those family jokes which isn't funny to anybody else or even, eventually, to the family who coined it, but which sticks. What mattered was the intent expressed in the name: this was a knowingly relaxed lunch. It was also a form of open house to which certain close family friends knew they were always invited. And so they would come.

It was at our kitchen table that I learnt the power of food and mealtimes. With a full plate in front of them, people would talk. They would drop on to their elbows and unload, both the good things and the bad, for my mother made her living as an agony aunt and was therefore considered both a good listener and a source of professional wisdom. There was no such thing as oversharing. Here, fuelled by those fish balls and bagels, they would be the most unselfconscious version of themselves. Oh, the stories they told. Sometimes we would talk about the food itself. I learnt the correct way to build a cream cheese and smoked salmon bagel. (The cheese is not a butter substitute, to be spread thinly. It is a pedestal for the salmon and so to be piled high, like a litter of cushions.) We would, between mouthfuls, discuss whether this week's chopped liver was as good as last week's. We would argue over who had dibs on that chocolate eclair. This was mostly a pointless argument; it was always my mother's, unless there were two of them. I understood that this life of the table mattered, and all of these things were a subject worthy of debate.

My relationship with both food and the life of the table had come to define a very personal and intense part of me, which eventually presented challenges. In 1999, when I was offered the job of restaurant critic for the *Observer*, I was both publicly overjoyed and privately ashamed. Naturally, I was delighted by the prospect of being paid to do what I had always done on my own dime: to wander from restaurant to restaurant, deciding whether it was worth anyone's time and money. But I also questioned whether making the personal so very public was seemly. I was thirty-two years old and finally established as a reporter, which I considered the most noble of the journalist's crafts. I had moved from soft arts and feature writing to sharper-edged news reporting. I was covering race crime and social policy. I had spent weeks at the Old Bailey sitting through the only war crimes trial ever to be held in the UK, and, for a while, dug around in the workings of the intelligence services until the British Government's D Notice committee, which polices the line between the media and national security, had told my editor to rein me in. I wore these things as a badge of honour. And now? Well now I was to write about the quality of a custard tart or the precision roasting of a loin of venison. I love custard tarts. I adore venison. But really?

I told a friend, a highly respected restaurant critic of many years' standing, that I would do the job for a few years and then return to 'proper' journalism.

I blush at the thought. What a staggeringly pompous thing to say, and how very wrong. All writers need a subject and in the world of food and restaurants I had found mine. The lesson I had learnt as a child at the family kitchen table over Fick and Porridge, that food and eating can take you anywhere, was to be repeated in adulthood. The subject of what we eat, I realised, is not just about how things taste. It is about memory and emotion, about love affairs and sex, and the two together. It is about family and education, the environment and agriculture. I remained a reporter, investigating the tangled politics and economics of food supply chains and national health policy. It led to a lengthy stint as a TV reporter for *The One Show* on BBC1, for whom I made over 150 short reports. I came to love the ones which showed us exactly where our food comes from: not just the airy, touchy-feely, niche artisan stuff of farmhouses and kitchen tables – although there was a bit of that – but the complex large-scale business of freezing a pea crop within forty-five minutes, or harvesting carrots in the middle of the night, when it is good and cold. I skimmed across a silvery Morecambe Bay at dawn's low tide to fish for brown shrimps, and stood in a tank with a massive farmed halibut in my arms as it was milked for its sperm. It was a varied life.

It was also superb experience for what was to come next. I had long been an occasional feature writer for *Observer Food Monthly*, my newspaper's supplement with the exceptionally literal title. In 2010, I was asked if I would write a column for the front of *OFM*, as it has come to be known. The column's name told me everything I needed to know: it would be called 'The Happy Eater'. It was to be a column about all aspects of food and eating written by a man who likes his dinner. And his lunch. And his breakfast. And any other meals he might be able to slip in between. What's more, it would be defined by a second column on the next page by the great American writer Ariel Leve. Hers would be called 'The Fussy Eater' and would chronicle the life of someone who was somewhat more suspicious of what she was being fed.

We set out our respective stalls right from the start. Ariel's first column was about how picky she could be when it came to eating sushi. Mine was about my fondness for the scuzziest of restaurants, the ones without velvet drapes and cut crystal. As I said, 'Denying yourself an edible pleasure just because you couldn't safely remove someone's appendix in the room in which it was prepared seems just plain foolish, not to mention self-defeating.' And so it began.

Ariel wrote wittily about American barbecue as if it was some dreadful cult; I wrote about how everything can be improved by the addition of bacon. She described her commitment to eating superfoods; I dismissed superfoods as anti-scientific cobblers. She wrote about how much she hated watching people eat in public; I wrote about the joys of dropping my lunch down my shirt. It was a classy double act, but one with a shelf life. An enthusiast like me has endless directions in which to go. For us the world is one big table, forever laid. It's all about more and seconds and 'yes please'. The fussy eater lives a more reduced life at that table. They're simply not as interested. So it proved. Within a couple of years, the fussy eater handed back her sterilised knife and fork. Ariel Leve had other great writing projects requiring her attention.

But the happy eater? I pushed on.

It's in the nature of a column written for a newspaper supplement that some of them would be tagged to events in the news. There was a debate around the rights and wrongs of tipping in restaurants. For the record, I argued that tipping should be scrapped altogether and restaurant staff should simply be paid a proper, reliable wage like people in other service industries. There was the allegation that the then prime minister, David Cameron, had, while a student, spent an interesting night with a pig's head. (Look it up.) Those columns date quickly.

But many more of them have ranged far and wide across the edible landscape in a less time-fixed manner. Now, collected together in a single volume, I like to think of it as a fatly stocked larder. Here are essays on why the messiest of dishes can also be the ones that taste the best, or why the secret to flavour lies in giving ingredients lots of time together. There are a few columns about restaurants, which, after all, are my specialist subject. I write about the dishes that professional kitchens do so well and those they do terribly badly. Lesson: you'll probably make a better apple crumble at home than any chef could ever make you in a restaurant. There's another piece about the joys of people watching at the table and one on why certain dishes stay in the memory and others do not. I tackle the thorny issue of Christmas food from all angles, which means I'm big on useful advice. Take it from me: the world won't end if you don't make a dozen side dishes, and for God's sake don't compare your Christmas to Nigella's, because that way madness lies. I also allow myself to indulge in some bile and vitriol, because there are some things around food that make me grind my teeth and it's far better for my molars that I get it all out there. The happy eater is not always happy. But sometimes he's ecstatic.

Each of the forty columns in this collection is 600 words long. Generally, writers shouldn't show their workings in the margins, the grammatical carpentry that makes it fit together. Still, it's worth acknowledging that 600 words is delightfully concise. Certainly, baggy writing is neither welcome nor helpful. There is a famous saying, attributed to everyone from the Roman consul Cicero to John Locke, Benjamin Franklin and Mark Twain: 'I would have made it shorter if I'd had more time.' Whoever should get the credit, there's no doubt it applies here. Of all my regular columns, this has always presented the most interesting of challenges, one that lends itself to cooking metaphors: just how do you reduce an argument down to its most intense essentials? What is superfluous to the way it's presented? And will you need to wear a napkin while reading it? At which point I may have stretched those food and cooking metaphors a little too far, but you get the point. At times I have written about the joy of fat, but the columns themselves are never flabby.

Certainly, it means this collection is ideally engineered for a particular status. When I was a kid there was a special category of volume in my house: the loo book, so defined because it was browsable in the requisite time. There were half a dozen of them in our toilet downstairs at home. One was a collection of cartoons by Carl Giles of the *Daily Express*, for example. Another was a book with short entries on *How to Curse in Yiddish*, which obviously provided a useful education. I came to love the familiarity of those editions and flicked through them often when I had to be in there. I am too well-mannered to point out the connection between where food goes in and where it comes out, but certainly a 600-word column is pretty much the perfect length for a stay in that smallest of rooms. All I'll say is this: once you've read *Chewing the Fat* the first time round, you'll know exactly where it should live.

HOME COMFORTS

Messing Around

Recently I made a dreadful mess in the kitchen. It was delicious. I was looking for something to kick off a dinner party, and was musing on the Jewish Ashkenazi staple, egg and onion: crushed-up cooled boiled eggs with slow-cooked, then cooled fried onions. It's a soothing trip to the nursery or, better still, the small child's overheated sickbed.

I wanted to make a grown-up version. Instead of onions I used finely sliced spring onions. I added chopped salted anchovies. I dressed it with a serious vinaigrette, made with spoonfuls of nose-tickling Dijon mustard and mayonnaise and glugs of peppery olive oil. I can't pretend. It looked terrible. It looked like it had been pre-consumed, rejected by the body as not fit for purpose and returned to the bowl from the wrong direction. I hesitated. Could I really serve this?

Then I scooped some on to a cracker. Forgive a moment's boasting, but God it was good: the comforting back rub of the eggs remained, but now there was an insistent kick from the anchovies and the spring onion and the Dijon. It was the word 'compelling' fashioned

3

from ingredients. Soon my friends were scraping at the glaze.

It got me thinking. So much of the very best food is like this, which is to say a huge bloody mess. It lies on the plate or in the bowl, looking like something requiring the attentions of the emergency services or a swift burial. And yet, it tastes marvellous. I'd go even further and say that messy food rules. Messy food is where the satisfying stuff is. There's a Vietnamese chicken dish I make, full of fish sauce, heaps of black pepper and sugar and handfuls of sliced ginger. It ends up looking as though a lot of bleach will be required to tidy up the dun-coloured 'accident'. It tastes fabulous, a bash of salt and sweet and umami.

Think of the very best stews; of chillies and curries, of fish stews bursting with saffron or even just a winter salad heaped on a plate. It looks like something awaiting the composter. It tastes fabulous. I know I'm not meant to think like this; that, when a plate lands on the table, people like me are meant to nod sagely, and mutter about the artful way in which the ingredients have been introduced to each other like they were guests at a cocktail party humming with sexual tension. Supposedly we eat with our eyes first. And I understand that ambitious chefs have spent so long fretting over each element of a dish that they are then going to take extreme care in their positioning on the final plate. Of course they are. And I can't promise not to comment on artful presentation in the future. We all appreciate it when a bit of effort has been made.

But I know my heart will be with the messy plate-fuls and I think for good culinary reasons. Making ingredients taste of themselves is of course virtuous. But slamming them together with other ingredients so they become something else is where the real action is. Messy makes flavours talk to each other. Messy makes them bounce off each other. It works. Now do excuse me. I've got an appointment with the kitchen. I need to make something that will require an awful lot of cleaning up. In a good way.

Jar Head

A little while ago the Yorkshire-based herb and spice company Steenbergs held a competition to find the oldest unused packet of spices in anybody's cupboard. The winner: a pot of Sainsbury's pickling spices bought in 1975 for 19p. Clearly, we should celebrate such Olympic-standard procrastination. I'm sure they were planning to get round to their brilliant home pickling project, just as soon as they had rearranged the cutlery drawer. But for me that response was overlaid by something else: recognition.

For purely by coincidence, while Steenbergs was encouraging the nation to excavate their kitchen cabinets, we were also giving our own walk-in larder a clean out. I say 'we'. It was entirely my wife's doing. I was minded to let sleeping condiments lie. Two of my unbending rules for a happy life: never look under a teenager's bed and never, ever mess with the kitchen cupboards.

But she was determined. And so the great work began. I stood by and watched as the shelves were emptied on to kitchen surfaces, which were quickly covered with a Manhattan of bottles and jars of ancient vintage. In the process it forced me to acknowledge all my unrealised ambitions as a domestic cook. My desire to be an endlessly inventive kitchen warrior with a seemingly boundless repertoire, piled up unceremoniously before me.

There were the jars of buttercup-yellow preserved lemons, and the dinky pots of harissa paste, the colour of coagulating blood, from the period when I was determined to explore the wilder shores of the Levantine culinary tradition. There were things called 'marmalade' which didn't involve oranges, and pitch-black pastes made from damsons which I seem to recall needing for my home experiments in neo-rustic British nose-to-tail eating. And don't get me started on the Asian stuff: the fermented bean pastes with endless permutations of chilli and dried shrimp; the misos of ever darkening shades; the rice wines and soys and vinegars.

Some of these had been opened. I peered inside to find a few with a deep dimple where I had sampled this new genius purchase and then realised I didn't have a clue what to do with it. Others had developed a furry mould so thick I didn't know whether to scoop them out or stroke them and get them baptised. And then there were those – oh the shame – where the seal hadn't even been broken.

Obviously, I should beat myself up here over the disgusting waste, and I do. It doesn't matter how long it takes to throw something away. Waste is still waste. But even more than that I mourn all those dishes that could have been. They were not undermined by lack of ingredients. I reckon I had even accumulated the makings for a couple of Yotam Ottolenghi's simpler recipes. They were undermined by lack of commitment.

I'm sure when I bought the myriad jars I meant it. I really was going to become a different kind of cook. I really was going to stop making the same old things I always made. But I was going to become that different cook tomorrow. Or perhaps the day after that. Or next week. And all of a sudden, it's six years later and you can't find the Marmite for the tubs of ras el hanout spice mix. But being brought face to face with all those unused products has stiffened my resolve. I will do better. I will be a more adventurous cook. And I will start all this a week next Thursday.

Oink

When I make my favourite pork and chorizo stew I start by searing off lumps of chorizo until it's caramelised and sticky and the paprika-coloured oil is running. Then I stand over the pan and eat half of it with my fingers until I have to cook some more. I begin a braised shoulder of lamb in this way too, for I think cured pig products add something to meat dishes of all varieties. Of course, it's also a fine addition to cheese on toast. The first thing I do when I make braised peas and lettuce, a lovely vegetarian dish, is chop two rashers of streaky bacon. I make a fine Vietnamese noodle and seafood soup. Obviously, what a fish soup needs is, you know, some pancetta. I add crisp-fried flakes of Parma ham to flageolet beans with olive oil and Parmesan, and think the one ingredient that really makes Savoy cabbage with apples fly is, well, bacon.

None of this is grandstanding for the sake of a cheap laugh. It is an accurate description of the food I cook. As far as I can see there is no savoury dish that can't be improved by the application of a little pig. I have, for years, been rude about restaurants in the Black Country, where my wife is from, but I forgive it almost everything for being home to the pork scratching, that virtuous combination of crackling, deep-fried fat and salt. I love Lardo di Colonnata, the cured creamy-white back fat of the pig, to be served very thinly sliced on hot toast so it starts to melt.

I eat ears and tails and cheeks and spleens. In Szechuan restaurants I eat livers gong bao and the mellifluously named flower-exploded kidneys. In French bistros I order andouillette, that gnarly French tripe sausage which smells and tastes like the farmyard before the farmer has bothered to clear away what the animals have left behind. And oh, for pork belly, a passion of mine so heated and developed there is probably a programme at the Priory specifically designed to deal with it. My name is Jay, and I am powerless in the face of pork belly. That crackling, which crunches dangerously between the molars. That long-cooked fibrous meat, and between the two a slippery layer of fat. I have tested so much of it on restaurant reviews that I try now only to order it when I am eating on my own time. I don't always succeed.

I love lamb. I bend the knee to beef. I have had a long and abiding relationship with chicken in all its forms. But the pig! Ah now, that is something different entirely. It has the skin that the others do not. It has the fat that the others do not. It takes a salt cure

10

in the way lamb or beef or chicken never can. It is the one ingredient no self-respecting cook could be without, and I'll punch anyone who argues with me. Frankly, when it comes to food, there are only two sorts of people: the ones who adore piggy products in all their fabulous variety, and everybody else.

Now obviously you can take things too far. In America, for example, it's possible to get bacon-flavoured gumballs. There's also bacon-flavoured dental floss and apparently even Squeez Bacon, a piggy-flavoured condiment. (Though I suspect the latter and Bacon Lube™, to help you 'keep it sizz-lin'', were only April Fool's jokes.) Best of all there's Mo's Bacon Bar, a slab of milk chocolate flavoured with applewood smoked bacon. It's chocolate, people. Flavoured with bacon! I call that progress. I wonder if they do mail order?

I Want It Now

I was born in 1966, from which vantage point the present was the unimaginable future. All I knew for certain was that life would be better half a century hence, more exciting and at the very least much shinier. Back then I imagine my hopes for the future involved hover cars, interplanetary travel and digital watches. And credit where it's due: the digital watches were fantastic.

But I'm older now. Going abroad for my holidays once a year takes it out of me, before I even consider the hassle of interplanetary travel. And I don't need a hover car. No, what I really want is a bit of help in the kitchen. Proper help of the sort we all had the right to expect would have arrived by now, but which hasn't. I don't want a machine to do the cooking for me. I like cooking. But there are a few gadgets which someone somewhere has forgotten to invent. Now it's the future, it's time someone dealt with this.

First up I want a fishbone magnetiser. Bloody obvious idea: it's a device which first magnetises the bones left behind in fish fillets, and then simply pulls them out so you don't have to stand over the fillets with a pair of tweezers pin-boning the damn things. I want to be able to stand and listen to the gentle sucking noise each filament-like bone would make as it was pulled from the flesh, and marvel at what a great place the twenty-first century is for cooks.

I also want a prawn peeler. I saw one once, a brilliant industrial-scale machine which sorted tiny Morecambe Bay shrimps, then put them on a miniature Ferris wheel so a perfectly calibrated suction device could pull the shells clear. I want a domestic version of one of those, so I don't ever have to swear again when I rip a shrimp or prawn in half because my fingers are too fat and clunky or I don't know my own strength.

Perhaps you think I'm overcomplicating the kitchen. Well, how about this one, then. I want a safe mandolin. That's all. A properly safe mandolin. Not one that only slices your hand open once for the ten times a standard mandolin mutilates you. I want a mandolin that never, ever slices your hand open, however staggeringly stupid you happen to be, because it turns out that life in the twenty-first century is seriously complicated with lots of distractions. And while we're at it, can I have a tin opener that sucks out the oil or brine around tuna, so it doesn't go all over my hands or the work surface every time I open one? No, I have no idea how this will work. It will probably involve tubing and a pump. All the good

13

things do. You work out the details. I'm blue-skying the future here.

But the main thing I want is a self-cleaning hob. A self-cleaning oven is all well and good: turn it up to max and run away while the gunk incinerates. But a self-cleaning hob, especially after I've done sausages, or a casserole, or a sausage casserole, would be a serious piece of work. I don't care if it comes courtesy of a lid with brushes and water jets that you simply close down, or one of those slightly needy-looking robots they were always demonstrating on *Tomorrow's World*. Just get it done. I'm fed up with cleaning the hob. The future is here. It's now. And I'm waiting.

Slow Down

Put the words 'Express' and 'Cooking' into Amazon and you get forty-two pages of book listings including, most prominently, *Nigellissima: Instant Italian Inspiration*, *Ainsley Harriott's Gourmet Express 2* (there was a first volume? Who knew?) and Liz Franklin's *Express Meals: 175 Delicious Dishes You Can Make in 30 Minutes or Less*. (Less? LESS? It should be fe . . . oh, never mind. But honestly, if you're being so bloody quick about the food couldn't you have used the extra time to brush up your grammar?) The words 'Quick' and 'Cooking' produce over a hundred pages of listings, including *Quick and Easy Vegan Slow Cooking* (Eh? What?) while 'Easy' and 'Cooking' produces an equal deluge with contributions from Rachel Allen, Lorraine Pascale and Bill Granger. Meanwhile some bloke called Jamie is promising to get dinner on your table in less time than I spend hiding in the bog in the morning.

For God's sake, people, stop. Or at the very least, slow down a little. Put down the spatula. Step away from the stove. Yes, of course, I know we all lead busy lives. Look up a picture of me on the internet. There's plenty of them, not all of them flattering. Do you think that hair looks after itself? It's so high-maintenance it has its own online diary. But even so there has to be time for cooking, or at the very least an understanding that it is not merely a means to an end, but an end in itself. I cook therefore I am.

This is never more so than in the colder months. Spring and summer are, of course, great for food, but oh aren't they self-satisfied. It's all asparagus this, and morels that. But when autumn shades into the sharp crack of winter the proper down-and-dirty stuff happens. And as with all the really good things in life, if something's worth doing it really is worth doing slowly. Or to put it another way, this is the season of the mighty braise. In the past I have described the glorious things that happen when you take a shoulder of lamb and sear it off, and then cook it long and slow in a bucket of red wine flavoured with onions, celery, carrots, garlic, chorizo and a scoop of brown sugar, as 'alchemy'.

Alchemy makes it sound inexplicable and unfathomable. Granted, the best food experiences do have a bit of that going on. Proper cooking charms. But in reality it's just chemistry. The shoulder is a bit of the animal which works hard and is thus striated with connective tissue; cook it long and slow enough and the collagen starts to break down. Meanwhile the cellular

16

structure of the vegetables collapses in the heat, and a little osmotic pressure allows for an exchange of salts. But the really great thing about all this is that it isn't 'Express!' or 'Quick!'. It takes patience. It takes stamina. It takes commitment. I would also say that, while it isn't exactly brain surgery, nor is it completely 'Easy!'. You need to know a few things. You need to know how to build a braising liquor; how to rest the meat at the end and the best way to strain and reduce that liquor to turn it into a sauce without letting it pass from rich to bitter. What matters, though, is the impact of all this on your house. Perhaps you go out for a stroll. And when you return the hall smells of great intentions. It is a promise, kept. It is commitment shown. It is something you will never, ever get from the words express, quick or easy.

Due Process

I bloody love processed food. Here's my favourite summer processed pork belly dish. In an oven pan I sauté chorizo, onions and carrots, then deglaze with red wine. I reduce by half, top up with chicken stock and chuck in some brown sugar. I bring it to a simmer and then put in a big square of pork belly. I cover it with foil and put it into a low oven for four hours. Once it's cooked I let it cool a little, wrap it in cling film and put it in the fridge overnight, under a weighted baking tray so it is pressed. The next day I slice it up into inch-thick pieces, and put those on to a smoking barbecue for a couple of minutes each side, until the meat is bronzed and the fat is crisped, and the air smells of all the thoroughly good piggy things.

I know what you're thinking. (Apart from: I wants me some of that pork belly.) You're thinking: that's not processing. That's home cooking. But what's the difference? Count the stages: the sautéing, the deglazing, the braising, the cooling, the wrapping, the pressing, the cutting, the grilling. If that's not a process I don't know what is.

This is not mere semantics. Clumsy food campaigners

and journalists, the ones who declare themselves committed to the detail of what we eat, seem far less committed to detail when it comes to the language they deploy. Because if they had to accept it's not all black and white, that there are good processes and bad processes, they would start to topple off their self-built soapboxes. As the brilliant food historian Rachel Laudan has put it, 'The proportion of our calories that come from "natural" foods is very small. Meat, milk, grains, sugar, vegetables are normally consumed only after chopping, grinding, pounding, evaporating, heating, and so on. That is true as far back in human history as we can go.'

It is the processing of raw ingredients which enabled us to extract from them the nutrition we needed as swiftly as possible so we could get on with doing the more interesting things that make us human. Whenever I hear a pursed-lipped food campaigner announce that we should eat only things our grandmothers would recognise, two thoughts occur: firstly, that my grandmother was a lousy cook and I'd fight to keep her away from the kitchen; and secondly, that she had to spend an awful lot of time in that kitchen to get anything done.

What's more, many processes have virtues. As Dariush Mozaffarian of Tufts University's Friedman School of Nutrition Science and Policy pointed out at the 2015 Aspen Ideas Festival, 'You get far more lycopene from tomato paste than raw tomatoes.' As lycopene, which gives tomatoes their colour, has various health benefits, that's a good thing. Then there's freezing, which preserves the nutritional value of vegetables far better than leaving them first on the supermarket shelf and then in your kitchen for days on end. And of course there are the gastronomic considerations. What would Asian food be without soy sauce, XO sauce, miso paste and the rest, all of them the result of a glorious process?

There are, of course, crappy processed foods: the ones with too much sugar or the wrong kinds of fats, or which get finished in the deep fat fryer. But even then, they're only bad if eaten too regularly. Tricky thing, discourse. But surely we're smart enough to use language properly? Surely we can debate without oversimplifying? Now then, who wants some of my processed pork belly?

FILTHY HABITS

Eating Dangerously

Greedy people like me are not, by nature, terribly fastidious when it comes to food. The imperative of eating just doesn't allow for it, not when you are the kind of person who picks the crispy bits off the bottom of the greasy pork roasting tin. The morning after the dinner of the night before. Or who, when they think no one is looking, will steal the folds of bronzed chicken skin left behind on the plates of others cursed with meaner appetites. I work on the assumption that food – and, by association, the restaurant that serves it – has to be trying bloody hard to kill you. Eating is not something you need insurance for. So denying yourself an edible pleasure just because you couldn't safely remove someone's appendix in the room from which it was prepared seems just plain foolish, not to mention self-defeating.

The fact is that in all the years that I have been eating professionally I have never suffered food poisoning, and that's not because I restrict myself to the sort of velvet-swagged gastro palaces where intense young men in box-fresh latex gloves prepare roast swan. When I am eating on my own dime, which, as a greedy man, I do an awful lot, I am far more likely to be drawn to the sort of joint obsessive compulsives would call scuzzy and I would call characterful.

An example: a while back I gave a glowing review to a cheap Szechuan restaurant which did marvellous things with piles of rustling dried chillies, salt and peppercorns. After the review was published readers, made of less stern stuff than I, sent me links to stories about the restaurant's conviction for contravening health and safety regulations.

Now honestly, I don't make light of the damage or distress acute food poisoning can cause. Death really is no fun. A vigorous health and safety regime is vital. But I would also be lying if I claimed this revelation changed my view of the restaurant in question. Indeed, I think it adds to the experience. Certainly, when I'm out of the country I know full well that if I want the real edible thrills I'm not going to find them in the places heavy with starched linen and glinting crystal-ware. I've spent a slab of time in Los Angeles over the years, and it is an extraordinary food town – but only at the cheaper end of the market. For the good stuff you have to go to the smoky barbecue restaurants in Koreatown where someone in filthy overalls may well be trying to clear the overflow from the ceiling pipes, but where the charcoal-grilled short rib will taste like nothing you have eaten anywhere else. Or you have

24

to visit the taqueria at Central Market in the heart of Hispanic-dominated Downtown, where heavyset guys with thick, tattooed forearms will load shreds of seared pig kidney into tacos, slather them with hot sauce and a spritz of lime juice and watch you admiringly as you down the lot.

Am I boasting about this? Absolutely, for the picky eater needs to know what they are missing; needs to know that because of some childish compulsion they have narrowed their experience of the world. Mostly it comes down to this. When people like me have a mouthful of blistering Thai curry from the greasy-tabled cafe on the corner, or are nibbling a black and crusted Tandoori lamb chop from the Pakistani eating house down the street, the last thing we are thinking about is whether it will kill us. Instead, we feel completely and utterly alive.

My Dirty Laundry

Recently, in a restaurant, I saw something astonishing. It's not an uncommon something; I see it regularly. It just always astonishes me. What I saw was a middle-aged man in a white shirt, rising from a table, having finished dinner. And there was not a single sauce stain on him. Not a drip or smear, not a dollop or skid mark. It was just one crisp snowfield of pristine linen.

How, in the name of all that is holy and quite a few things that aren't, does this work? Because I seem completely incapable of leaving a table without everyone being able to read, from the full Jackson Pollock across my chest, exactly what I've just had for my tea. Ah, so you went for the bouillabaisse followed by the cheesecake in raspberry coulis, did you? Oh, so it was curry night, was it? Well, of course, that whole linguine vongole thing is tricky, isn't it.

You're telling me. I have measured out my life in ruined shirts; in turmeric stains the colour of that medicinal iodine we called yellow magic that was swabbed on to our scabbed knees at primary school. I have lived through the era of chicken tikka masala and the chilli oil years. Most people view a dish of handmade pasta with a long-simmered sauce of heritage tomatoes as representative of the eternal verities of Italian peasant life; I see it as one calamitous laundry bill.

I am used to my beloved looking me up and down from the other side of the table and mouthing the words 'well done' because I have somehow got through the main course unscathed, like I'm six and managed to dress myself unaided. She always mouths too soon. Because only minutes later the chocolate sauce will doubtless cascade down me like a mudslide.

In my more fragile moments, I like to think of myself as a victim of heredity, because my late mother was also incapable of not wearing her lunch. 'Oh look,' she would say, dabbing at her blouse with a moistened napkin, 'I've schtunked,' swiftly turning the Yiddish for stinker into something much more onomatopoeically descriptive. Then again, she had the excuse of a sizable shelf which, even in my chunkier days, I cannot claim. She wore a lot of floral prints which covered a multitude of stains.

Being more generous to myself, I reach for another explanation. I make a mess of my clothes at the table because I take the business of eating seriously. The ones who manage not to spill everything down their shirts are obviously not doing food properly. They must be half-filling every spoon's bowl. They must lean in over their barely laden fork, top lip trembling with the effort. Me? I'm shovelling the food away, like a rescue worker clearing the debris in search of survivors.

There are even some occasions when I revel in my slovenliness. If I rise from a meal in a Chinese restaurant and the paper tablecloth around where each dish stood doesn't look like a blast zone of scattered food, then I regard myself as having in some way failed. And if I glance across at someone else's table and it's pristine, then I involuntarily mouth the word 'amateur'. The interplay of bowl, chopstick and Chinese cooking demands mess. And yet the shirt stains still bother me. I like to think of myself as a man of the world. I like to think of myself as elegant and mature. In truth I am just one massive splatter of lunch waiting to happen.

Taking Control

There is a moment in the pitch-perfect 1987 movie *Broadcast News*, about the television news industry, which has always spoken to me. Peter Hackes, playing the veteran news executive he once was, confronts the argumentative producer Jane Craig, played by Holly Hunter. 'It must be nice to always believe you know better,' Hackes says. 'To always think you're the smartest person in the room.' Hunter blinks back the tears. 'No,' she whispers, 'It's awful.'

Oh Holly, I know exactly what you mean. For here is the ugly confession: in the domestic kitchen, I am that person. I try not to be. I try not to interfere when other people are cooking. I want to be a relaxed, genial soul who knows that other people can cook and that I should let them get on with roasting the chicken or making the gravy and be thoroughly appreciative. But if I just happen to be walking through the kitchen and just happen to pass the stove and just happen to notice something isn't quite as it should be – that, say, the gravy is a thin, translucent outrage – I can't stop myself.

I am a model of politeness. Of course I am. I'll say

something like, 'Perhaps a knob of butter would help,' or 'Maybe you should turn up the burner and reduce it a little.' Or, 'FOR CHRIST'S SAKE WHAT THE HELL ARE YOU DOING YOU INCOMPETENT NUMPTY?' No, hang on. Those are the words that are actually going through my head while I'm saying the polite things. As dear Holly says, it's awful.

I know I am not alone in this. One friend told me he had once been admonished for 'trying to edit' a colleague's sandwich. My sympathies are entirely with the editor. His co-worker was doubtless making a truly dreadful sandwich, a calamity slammed between two slices of bread. He was merely attempting to save him from himself. Once, during a TV shoot, I was chastised for my knife skills. When I challenged my accuser, they said, 'But you were doing it wrong.' So I do know exactly what it's like. And yet I still don't seem able to stop myself meddling in other people's cooking.

I could tell you I only want to help, that I'm doing it out of kindness, but even I recognise I'd deserve a slap for that. Because in truth, the only person I'm trying to help is myself. I'm employed to travel the country in search of restaurants offering good things to eat and sometimes, despite my best endeavours, I fail. I have to eat terrible things. If I'm now standing in a kitchen and can see that, unless I intervene and quickly, I'm going to be made to eat something which is a disaster of a nightmare of a travesty, of course I'm going to attempt to change the outcome. I'm going to work to make things better. It's who I am.

But there's something else. Part of cooking's appeal to me is that it gives us a sense of control over the world around us, when everything else is chaos. We bend ingredients to our will. And it's very hard to relinquish that control. Even when you're wrong. Because sometimes I am. There. I've said it. I'm pretty good in the kitchen, but I'm not that good. Put me in a restaurant kitchen surrounded by serious pros and I won't say a bloody word. But in the home kitchen, most of the time I do know what I'm doing. Still, I recognise I need to come up with a solution to the issue, one that makes everything better for everybody. After much careful thought I have. It is this: if you're cooking for me and I'm in the kitchen with you, please don't screw up. See, it's really very simple.

Free Love

There's only one thing better than a Danish pastry and that's a free Danish pastry. There was a time when such things didn't feature greatly in my life, but now Denmark's fancy bakery chain Ole & Steen has begun rolling itself out across London and everything has changed. As well as reasonable coffee and a fine line in open sandwiches, they will insist on offering platters piled high with chopped-up pieces of their finest bakery product to nibble on for free while you wait: flaky pastry, a filling of lightly spiced apple, decorated with a scribble of white icing. What's not to like?

This has given me cause to think deeply about one of the most profound issues facing those of us who eat food: the etiquette around snaffling free samples. The Danes are famously polite, trusting souls. Doubtless, at home their customers pick a single piece, take their coffee and go. But I'm not Danish, and nobody has ever referred to me as Jay 'Restraint' Rayner. Frankly, if no one's watching too closely, I can scarf the equivalent of a whole Danish in the gap between saying, 'A white Americano, please,' and 'Thank you'.

In this I am aided by the fact that the servers in Ole & Steen are busy. Plus, it's not their cake, so what the hell. It can be much harder in, say, branches of Yorkshire cake-mongers Betty's, where the freebies are often displayed under glass cloches. It takes both real commitment and shamelessness to lift the lid and grab handfuls of Fat Rascals, while being stared down by one of Betty's finest, a mere pursed lip away from a Harrogate tut.

But the trickiest of all is the knit-your-own-yoghurt farmer's market, full of greedy sods fondling rare-breed chickens. These businesses invariably belong to the stallholders themselves. Here, a free sample is meant to convert to a sale. And boy is it hard to feign exactly the right expression of cheese-obsessed interest as your fingers reach out for the hunks of overpriced Gruyère, when you have not the slightest intention of buying any. Hard but, trust me, not impossible.

There is also the free sample hierarchy to navigate, for not all freebies are born equal. At the bottom you get those flogging cold-pressed rapeseed oil, by suggesting you dip swabs of badly made bread into glistening bowls of the stuff. The product may be great, but a mouthful of grease is not my idea of a good Sunday morning out. Just above that are the bespoke fruit stands trying to offload gnarly varieties of apple you've never heard of, by piling slices into trays. Generally, it's impossible to get to these because they're surrounded by anxious parents, their children still strapped into over-engineered buggies, who are desperately trying to shovel free fruit down their little darlings' gullets.

So instead you head to the chilli jam stands proffering crackers you'd never dream of eating otherwise, followed by the stalls shifting artisanal hummus like tile grouting, courtesy of mini breadsticks. Above them are the cheesemongers and, finally, for those with a taste for the animal, the holy grail of all free samples: the sausage stands, the coarse-cut porkers sliced into thick discs. The key here is to learn how to hold multiple cocktail sticks in your hand at once, so you hit three or four pieces with one pass. And if that all sounds like too much trouble just give up and head back to that Danish coffee shop. Trust me: it's as easy as taking free cake from a bakery.

Bad Dad

Being a nutritional role model for your kids is tough when you're a greedy-guts with all the self-restraint of a hungry lioness with her head stuffed into the carcass of a recently downed zebra. I was thinking about this recently as I was hiding my stash. As ever, it was the hard stuff: a bag of sherbet lemons, bars of M&S Swiss milk chocolate and a packet of Mr Porky scratchings. The hiding place is the corner of the top shelf of our walk-in food cupboard. For years it has been the perfect place to hide my filth. I was the only one who could see what was there.

And then I realised: no more. My fourteen-year-old son is almost my height, and apparently gifted with the wisdom of the ancients. He now knows and sees EVERYTHING. This was confirmed a little while later when he barged in on my wife and me in the living room, as we hurriedly tried to hide the tattered evidence of the chocolate we had just devoured in front of the telly. He didn't even look at us. 'I know you've had chocolate,' he said. 'I know where you keep it.' He might as well have announced that he had located something boasting three speeds and made of washable latex under the marital bed.

Tricky business, this parenting lark. We appoint ourselves custodians of our kids' bodies and then keep watch like prison camp guards: on their teeth, the nutritional intake they need for their bones and bodies. No, you can't have sweets. That glass of Coke is just pure sugar. Get off the computer and go outside and play. I said just ONE custard cream. Step away from the biscuit tin. I said, step away . . .

We are right to do this. It really is a part of the job description. The problem is that we are the least qualified people for that job. We are like bent vice squad coppers, who bust addicts for heroin possession only to tie on the tourniquet and shoot up ourselves once we've clocked off. We rampage through a box of Celebrations once the kids are in bed, then hide the evidence if we hear small footsteps on the stairs; we stuff late-night crisp packets into our pockets hurriedly. And yes, I am making the personal a universal. I have to assume I'm not alone in this. I have to assume you are all the same as me, otherwise how could I live with myself?

We do, of course, have a rationale. The mere fact that we have reached the cool, sunlit pastures of adulthood with all our own teeth intact and minus a diagnosis of type 2 diabetes means we have learnt self-restraint. Hurrah for us! Let's celebrate with Ben and Jerry's chocolate fudge brownie ice cream from those pots we keep hidden at the back of the freezer behind the Tupperware tubs of leftovers. Or perhaps with just another glass of that really good value Chablis from Aldi.

That's the reality of most middle-aged parental hypocrisy: we lecture our kids on eating sweets. We keep their hands out of the biscuit tin. And yet too many nights of the week we pull the cork on something eminently quaffable. This, I suppose, is life. And parenting. We do the very best we can, which never feels quite good enough. We feel gloomy about it. And hence we feel the need to comfort ourselves. Oh sod it. The kids are in bed. Just another glass. It can't hurt. Can it?

Microplane Speaking

Being a fully paid-up member of the acutely taste-
ful, exquisitely nuanced, belly-obsessed bourgeoisie
is a dreadful struggle, and never more so than when
summer holidays approach. For with the anticipation
– of long lunches on bougainvillea-scented terraces
with sea views, of chilled glasses of rosé as dusk falls
– comes The Fear. It is the stomach-churning fear of
the, oh God, ill-equipped kitchen.

This year we have rented a house in Greece, and
while I have flicked endlessly through the online
photographs, imagining myself inhabiting the scene,
it is the pictures of the kitchen I have lingered over,
in search of signs. Except there never are any, because
images like this are an exercise in advanced OCD.
Any clutter, any object which might leave a clue, has
been tidied away. I'm delighted there's a wine fridge,
obviously. But what I really need to know is this: what
are the kitchen knives like?

It's a stupid question. Kitchen knives in rentals
are always crap. They are never bought to be sharp
and perfectly weighted. They are bought to look like
kitchen knives, not to actually be them. I therefore

start making a list of the things I'll need to take with me, to make this the dream holiday that I've been playing out in my mind.

Firstly, there really will have to be those kitchen knives from home. And while we're at it, what about a good chopping board? Too many rentals appear to think that glass chopping boards, which produce the sound of nails down a blackboard when the blade gets through the onion, are a good idea. They aren't. A modest non-glass one wouldn't go amiss, would it. And a cafetière. Sure, there's a coffee machine in the pictures but it will take me days to work out how to use one of those effectively. And don't get me started on bloody Nespresso machines and their knock-offs. The coffee always comes out lukewarm.

So yes, knives, a chopping board, a cafetière. And, of course, proper-sized mugs, instead of those dismal thimbles they always have. I need a bucket of coffee in the morning. I don't want to keep going back for refills. This is about my needs, and my needs are extremely detailed. Maybe I should take a Microplane. I don't actually own one at the moment, but perhaps now is the time to get one just so I can take it with me on holiday, along with a really good corkscrew, a proper pair of tongs and . . .

Which is when I begin to understand the attraction of caravanning. You don't have to take kitchen equipment with you, because the kitchen is always there. Fabulous. Which is also when the words 'what have I become?' flit across my mind. If buying a caravan is the answer it must be a pretty stupid question. Where's my sense of adventure? Where's my spirit of improvisation?

I once watched a trailer for *Gordon Ramsay: Uncharted*, his series for National Geographic. He is seen climbing trees freestyle, scaling cliff faces and driving motorbikes along needle-thin mountain paths; I do hope nothing awful happens to him. He's also seen cooking with the barest bits of kit: sticks, flints, a machete and a barely sublimated fear of male inadequacy. I thought to myself: 'Maybe I should be more like Gordon.'

Finally, I came to my senses. Anything which makes me conclude I should imitate Gordon Ramsay is a lost cause. It's back to plan A. I don't need that many clothes for a good summer holiday. I don't really need shoes or books. But believe me, I really do need some good sharp knives. It's time to get packing.

Come Away with Me

It is August, the month of my great social experiment, or the summer holidays as other people call them. Here's how it works. Each year we book a large house with too many rooms for my own family. It could be anywhere but this year it happens to be in Spain; the Spanish stay up later than the Italians, and the food is less exhausting than in France. Then we invite other families to join us. There is one condition, beyond us all liking each other. They don't just have to be willing to do their share of the cooking. They have to be eager to do so.

And then the social experiment begins. Because you can learn more about a friend by cooking alongside them than through almost any other common pursuit. Certainly, you can learn more than by simply eating their food. When it comes to character assessments what matters is not the ends, but the means that got you there.

In the past I have cooked with people who were so slow at peeling potatoes that the desire to rip both implement and tuber from their hands shouting 'FOR GOD'S SAKE LET ME DO IT' was so strong, I had to leave the room and sit in the toilet with the door shut and the light off, rocking back and forth in the darkness hugging myself. I have felt my heart rate rise as a friend – I say friend; I mean someone I hope never to see ever again in my life – stood slugging rosé and telling a tiresome anecdote over searing steaks that were being ruined with each narrative beat of the pointless bloody story. I have watched someone put Marmite in the salad dressing. They winked at me while they did it, as though I were being let in on a secret. Yes, one of those dark, filthy secrets that you hope the tabloids will one day expose.

From cooking alongside someone, you can learn whether they are reliable and trustworthy. If we can get dinner for fourteen on the table together without fuss or bother, I know for certain that this is someone who will get me through the more dramatic events in life. Say, a hostage situation. From cooking alongside someone, you can learn whether they attend to the details of life; whether they sense the passage of time; whether they can refill a wine glass, keep an eye on the steaming clams so they haven't gone into the rubber stage, and spot that the gratin is on the edge of burning under the grill, all at once. By cooking alongside someone you can tell whether they are a good listener. Because so much of cooking is about listening to the sound your food makes. A good cook can hear well done long before others can smell it.

I will happily admit that I have gone from simply liking a friend to adoring them, based on their ability to be ready with the pasta for a multitude when I am ready with the sauce. If this sounds controlling on my part, then fine. Guilty as charged. Because really what I am looking for in a person I cook with, what I really want, is someone who enables me NOT to feel like a control freak. They have done everything that needs doing without me telling them to do it. In short, what I'm looking for from the people I cook with on holiday is for them to make me feel normal. Is that too much to ask?

I Am What I Am

Being a pervert carries with it risks, the most acute of which is exposure. Deviating from the norm is fine, unless everyone finds out. The only way to face this challenge is to be open; to be out and proud about exactly who and what you are. That is what I intend to do, right here and right now. I found the strength to do so after a consultation with my family or, to be more exact, some bitter piss-taking by my eldest son. He looked at what I was having for breakfast one day, shook his head and said, 'If only people knew . . .' For a moment I was afraid. What if people did find out? What then? Would my reputation be in tatters? Which was when I concluded that I had to be myself, that if I was honest and open nobody could hold anything over me.

So here it is: I adore burnt toast. I don't mean slightly darker than the way you like your toast. I mean black. Best of all is still-hot black toast with a smear of butter (the cheap spreadable kind) that fizzes into the holes on contact and then a bit of Marmite to dance with the acrid carbon notes. Sure, I don't NEED toast to be burnt. I can enjoy other sorts of toast. But I very much like it that way. It makes me happy.

You don't think that's especially transgressive, do you? Okay. How about this. I am a slut in the matter of spare ribs. I will eat any spare rib including – no, especially – those deep red ones the colour of the make-up used for 'red' Indians in racist Hollywood westerns. By which I mean the ones sold by cheap knock-off fried chicken shops in the more interesting urban areas. I like the massive hit of salt and sugar, the coating that goes so deep that you no longer have to worry about the provenance of the meat inside because it's been completely obliterated. It could be pork. It could be lamb. It could be Alsatian. Who the hell knows? Who cares? After a bucketful of cheap Hungarian Laski Riesling, not me.

Obviously, I am a major fan of quality ice creams. There is nothing like hand-churned buckets of the good stuff laced with ribbons of salt caramel or frozen fruit coulis. But on a hot summer's afternoon in a London park, with the local dogs dancing in the litter, there is simply nothing to beat Mr Whippy. There is something utterly compelling about that mixture of minimal dairy fats, vegetable oil and air. I am happy to pay for air.

In cinemas I buy popcorn. Of course I do. That's what you're meant to do. But it's not what I want.

I want those corn starch, fat and salt weapons of cardiovascular mass destruction sold as nachos alongside a bright orange 'cheese' whip which has about as much in common with cheese as my cat. Yes, I know it's bad food, in the way that the regime in North Korea is bad government. But I like the pungency. I barely ever buy it, for fear of being seen. The depths of my depravity would be understood. Well now I don't have to worry. It's all out there. Sure, I still adore the good stuff. Bring me the well-aged ribs of Highland long horns, the runny Bries de Meaux. I once asked Hugh Fearnley-Whittingstall what his guilty food secret was. He said: 'A frothy pint of ale and a Snickers from the fridge.' Really. Flavour aside, that is just so vanilla. The fact is every now and then I have needs. I'm sure you do too. And they will be satisfied.

HATE SPRINGS ETERNAL

My Life Is Not a Picnic

After 'Please come to my superhero-themed wedding' the most distressing leisure-time proposition in the English language has to be: 'Fancy a lovely picnic?' No, I don't. Picnics are never lovely. Picnics are where lunch goes to die. Yes, I know. I'm not meant to say this. Each summer, by convention, magazines are given over to gloriously photographed picnic features, many of which I have contributed to. And so a confession: every time I have done so, I have been colluding in one big fat lie.

We dream of a life that echoes the pages of the Boden catalogue, in which all women look good in a wrap dress, all men look fine with their top three shirt buttons undone, white-toothed children entertain themselves for hours and the elders of the tribe smile beatifically at everything about them as together we lay into a feast of such largesse the Greek gods themselves would have to invent a bunch of other gods just so they could thank them for their huge good fortune.

The reality? It's impossible to look elegant while sitting on a sloping hillside or beach, especially at my age. Bits of me are always trying to make a bid for freedom. Sod muffin tops; I'm packing half the cake counter at Greggs. The kids are either punching each other or poking a dead, maggot-infested bird with a stick, there's something from the wrong end of an animal caked on your shoes and Granny's going into advance stages of anaphylactic shock, having been stung by the wasp that got bored of divebombing the last mulched-up strawberries that didn't fall out of the picnic bag when it opened accidentally.

Ah yes, picnic food. It's awful, a waste of agriculture. For here is what no glossy supplement will ever tell you: the quality of an eating experience decreases in direct proportion to the distance it travels from its point of origin. Chicken wings are lovely straight out of the oven; after they've spent six hours festering in a warm Tupperware box, eating one is as much fun as chewing on one of Gollum's sweaty knee joints. Potato salad which had bite and a substance while cooling on your kitchen table ends up looking like it's taken a beating in a cement mixer and is now designed only for those without recourse to teeth.

Or there's worse: the host comes over all ambitious. There's a poached fish which is falling apart quicker than Michael Jackson's face, or a roast rib of beef which looks great but which is impossible to eat because nobody thought to bring a sharp enough knife with which to carve it. Or if they did it's impossible to carve while rested on your lap without performing an un-elective vasectomy. The cold drinks are warm, the hot drinks are tepid, the soft fruit is mashed, the hard fruit is bruised, the quiche looks like it's already been eaten and come back out the wrong way and even the filling of the pork pie has disengaged from the mother ship of its pastry shell. Only the grapes look like grapes. This is no consolation.

I like tables. And chairs. And rooms to put them in. I regard these things as progress. The last time us Jews were forced to eat al fresco it was because the Cossacks were coming. If I want the great outdoors while eating, I'll open a bloody window. You want a picnic? Good for you. I'm staying here in the kitchen, where the food tastes nice. Have a great summer.

Bloody Luxury

It's taken me a while to get there, but finally I've reached a conclusion: where food and drink is concerned, luxury is hell. This revelation came to me one Sunday morning, as I navigated the deformed miseries of breakfast in bed. It's meant to be the height of indulgence; the route to that little bit of pink-negligéed Barbara Cartland lurking within us all. You are supposed to rub your hands together with childish glee: ooh, a little eggy something on a tray. Instead, you can never get comfortable, the tray is unstable on the bed and you know you'll be hoovering crumbs off the sheets for days. It becomes a trauma of sweaty crevices and butter-smeared pillows, and not in a good way. And don't even talk to me about the risks of Nutella stains. Other brands aren't available.

There are many examples of this. There are the dread words 'champagne reception'. One glass of champagne is fine. One glass is lovely. I adore a single flute, misty with condensation, the bubbles popping against your upper lip as you drink. But a whole damn night of it? It's a vile collision of gaseousness and tooth-stripping acidity, with only the promise of a headache within a couple of hours to remind you what a terrible idea it all was. Plus, nobody can ever afford the good stuff at these events, so what you end up drinking tastes like something you'd use to polish coins or ward off foxes.

Then there's the threat of an inspired chef taking you on a journey through the depths of their creativity via the medium of an eleven-course tasting menu. Shoot. Me. Now. It sounds great, doesn't it, this whole tasting menu thing. Away with the tyranny of dull old starters and dreary main courses. Who wants something as lumpen and uninspired as that, when you can have three and a half hours of itsy-bitsy tweezered miniaturism? Me. I want the lumpen and the uninspired. The truth is that few chefs have enough good ideas to sustain that many plates and if you do get something good, it's tiny and therefore gone far too quickly. Once, in California, I was served twenty-six minuscule courses by an infuriating chef who was trying to make a point. At the end he came out and said, 'Did I win?' If your goal was to make me despise you, then yes, chef, absolutely. Well done you.

I live in fear of fancy hotel afternoon teas, those assault courses of patisserie, finger sandwiches and bloating that leave you overloaded with carbs and facing up to the reality of a long, unstructured evening because dinner is now out of the question. And all eaten perched on the edge of an overstuffed sofa, your knees banging against an over-varnished coffee table the colour of Donald Trump. And I really do despair of overgenerous edible gifts. What the hell are you supposed to do with a whole side of smoked salmon or a leg of Jamón ibérico? On day one it's a joy. On day seventeen, its continued presence feels like a failure of character.

I know what you're thinking: that this is a disgusting display of self-indulgence; that to whine about too much champagne, too much Spanish ham and gargantuan afternoon teas in an age of austerity is obscene. You'd be absolutely right. So perhaps this should be seen as a service: I'm simply making it clear that the good things in life aren't actually good. They're awful. They're dreadful. Especially breakfast in bed. That really is a bloody nightmare.

Just Stop It

My dentist tells me that I grind my teeth at night. He says this is a very bad thing and needs to be remedied. Apparently the problem is tension, brought on by stress. Clearly I need less stress in my life. To make this happen I have decided to address all the things about restaurants that I truly hate; the atrocities I wish would disappear. These things may sound minor, but together they amount to a hurricane of tooth-blunting fury. My ability to chew meat properly depends upon all of it being dealt with.

Please stop taking my order without a notebook. I don't know you. I don't know whether you are Francesco the Famous Memory Man, or were off your tits last night on crystal meth and can now barely recall your own name. I don't trust you to remember what I ordered. Write it down.

All restaurants must install big enough tables to accommodate their small plate sharing menus. The small plates menu was your idea, not mine. Most tables can't manage more than four dishes, and you want us to order seven. And while we're at it, please stop sending dishes out 'when they're ready'. I am tired of not being able to remember if everything I ordered has been delivered. I'm bored of the potatoes arriving before the steak, of the steak arriving before the salad. It's convenient for the kitchen. It's not convenient for me. Stop it.

Stop it with granola too. Apart from at breakfast. Granola at breakfast is okay, but if I ever see it on a main course again, I shall open my mouth and point at my ground-down molars. It's ugly in there. Forget the jaws of hell. These are the jaws of Rayner. Also, please sort out the lighting. I am old. I dislike having to power up the torch on my phone to read the menu.

What is it with taking the bread plate away at the end of the starters? No restaurateur has ever explained to me why that happens, but still you do it. And while I'm on bread: unsalted butter? I mean, really! I don't want a mouthful of flavourless grease with my bread. You don't want people in your restaurant who dislike salted butter. They have feeble, over-sensitive palates. They will hate your food. And if they don't, I will. Oh, and put salt and pepper on the table. Who do you think you are? Nico bloody Ladenis?

Please stop putting the pages of wine lists inside plastic sleeves. It's cheap and feels nasty. How much does it cost to reprint them? And list bottles in price order from cheapest upwards. I love learning about the wines of the world, but not when I'm knackered and just want a sodding drink. I don't like having to hunt for something in my budget. And if I tell you I'll fill the wine glass myself I mean it. Tell your colleagues so I don't have to keep repeating myself. Don't you dare move my bottle to a table at the far end of the room. It's mine. I paid for it. I'll do with it as I like. And finally, don't you ever, ever, ever again give the bill to the only person on the table who happens to possess testicles. You have no idea who's paying for dinner. Put the bill in the middle of that table and walk away.

There. I'm done. And you know what? My teeth feel better already.

Swimming against the Tide

I live daily with the fear that, like Hector in Alan Bennett's *The History Boys*, I am 'not in the swim'. At the great dinner party of life, I'm on the children's table, a mere spectator on the grown-up fun. This is because, deep breath, I don't have a favourite gin. Yup, I know. If I were asked at a bar which gin I would like with my tonic, I would only stammer. But that's only the beginning. The truth is I don't have a favourite gin, because I hate ALL gin. As far as I'm concerned having a favourite gin would be like choosing a favourite war criminal, only with a greater impact on my life.

It's worse even than the time I admitted to not liking a negroni, that cruel and bitter slap of a cocktail, a taste for which is meant to mark you out as a mature sophisticate. Despite all the hype the negroni remains a niche drink. Even if I don't want to be part of the negroni drinking gang, there's surely another gang over there I can go hang out with.

But gin: today, that's everybody's drink. It's like bindweed: bloody everywhere. Tesco has its own-brand gin, as do Morrisons and Sainsbury's. Everybody has an own-brand gin. You probably have one too. Is it named after a character in a Guy Ritchie movie? Something like Copper Head or Lone Wolf or Conker? Many are. But being ubiquitous is not the same as being nice. I dislike the hit of juniper and the dank hit of undergrowth wrenched from a fox-soiled hedgerow. You call it the taste of 'botanicals'; I call it the taste of 'musty leaf matter'.

As the number of available gins grew, often marketed by cheery fellas who just happened to wear flat caps every day and keep their woollen trousers up with braces, ready to party like it's 1869, I became increasingly cynical. Gin production, I decided, was for people who want to enter the horny-handed world of 'artisanal food crafting' but can't be doing with all that filthy countryside business. Gin is something you can 'craft' in a city, around the corner from a good coffee shop and a ready supply of Korean chicken wings.

Can you smell my cynicism? It's nothing compared to what I stank of when I made the big discovery. As a man who writes about food and drink I'm meant to know things but, as ever, ignorance springs eternal. Until a year ago I hadn't quite clocked that often gin is just vodka to which stuff has been added. It is ruined vodka. Some gin producers don't even make the vodka. They buy it in, then they ruin it. That's tragic because I adore vodka; I love its crispness and its cleanness. It was when I was thinking about this vodka love that I realised the problem. Flowery, juniper-sodden gin is just too interesting, too multidimensional for me. I crave something duller, or at best a blank canvas upon which I can paint my own boozy story.

In this, I may be far less alone than I at first imagined. As I examined the gin world, I was struck by how much of it is marketed on tasting of something other than gin: there's quince gin and clementine gin. There's watermelon flavour and chocolate orange flavour and lemon drizzle cake flavour. There's Mystical Unicorn gin liqueur from Aldi, which apparently tastes of marshmallow and candy floss, and Parma Violet gin from Asda, which must taste of nightmares. What none of them can taste of is gin. Is it possible that most people don't actually like standard gin at all? Perhaps they just want to belong to a tribe? If so, then I'm happy to remain an outcast. You'll find me over in the corner, alone, nursing a vodka.

Losing Both Your Lunch
and Yourself

I will spare you the graphic details. Unless you are absurdly lucky, or party to a pact with the devil – send me over the paperwork; I'll happily sign – the last thing you need is detail. Whatever your name for the damn thing – the norovirus, the winter vomiting bug, a trip to the very jaws of fiery hell – you've been there, if not this season, then perhaps last season or the one before that. Along with death and taxes, a day or two gripping the porcelain is one of life's rare certainties. It came to me, as it did to you and you and you, just a few weeks ago.

For anybody with what might politely be called an enthusiastic approach to dinner time, and less politely might be called an instinct to greed, it can be a disconcerting experience. Not only do you lose your lunch. You lose the sense of self. Part of the trauma is its stealthy arrival, like high flat clouds spilling softly into a blue summer sky, so that you don't notice the change in the weather until the sun has finally been smudged away. It came to me over a snatched supper, late one night, at a bar. I ordered the food with enthusiasm. I always try to put my back into it. Quickly

I noticed that these dishes I so loved had become relentless, tiresome, an unwelcome part of the evening. Like the driver who puts their foot on the accelerator because they've noticed they're almost out of petrol, I began shovelling the food away as quickly as possible. To leave it uneaten would have been to acknowledge what my body had already clocked: all was not well.

And then, within a few hours, it begins. You ride the waves. You clutch the bed sheets. Even the most atheistic of us begin to wonder whether we have, in some way, offended the gods. Deliriously, we promise to make amends for our debauched behaviour if only this hell will lift. We will kick the pork scratching habit between meals. In fact, we'll eat nothing at all ever again from now on. How does that sound?

That is the truly bizarre bit about the experience: for a day or two, eating isn't just an uncomfortable thought; it's an impossibility. The me I know has gone. Most of the time, when I'm not eating, I'm thinking about what I will soon be eating. As I type, for example, there's lamb breast in the oven, braising. Once done I'm going to press it in the fridge for a few hours and then sear it off. I've been thinking about these breasts for days. I'm that kind of chap. I always have one of these fantasies on the go. Now, lying in bed, a deckhand on the good ship nausea, I try to fantasise. I think about crisp bacon. Frying bacon is the thing most likely to convert vegetarians. It's the test. Quickly I turn my head to the wall, as if trying to glance away from my own fat-slicked thoughts. The war of my gastrointestinal tract has further to run.

And then slowly, surely, it begins to subside. The waves soften and flatten. The tourniquet around the head loosens and drops away. Suddenly, rising from downstairs, you smell something: the high sooty tang of toasting bread. You think about smearing a little butter into its warm cracks, about the way it will melt. You think about Marmite and realise your body craves salt. It occurs to you that you might be better. And gently you whisper: hello me. God, but it's good to see you.

Dessert Parsley

Recently I was asked by a friend if I would help mount a war against tweezer food. You know the sort of thing: ingredients so eye-wateringly delicate that they could not possibly be placed on the plate using anything so blunt as fingers. My friend certainly made a good argument. Anything in this known universe worth eating, he said, would always be of a size that would render tweezers redundant. If you can't stuff it into your gob with your hands what's the point?

He's right. A while back I stood in the kitchen during service at Dabbous, the lava-hot, flog-your-granny-for-a-booking London restaurant, and watched mesmerised as each of the cooks withdrew from somewhere deep inside their aprons a pair of tweezers. The way their fingers moved, those guys could have performed keyhole surgery on me; if ever I elect to get the snip I won't bother with BUPA. I'll just book a table there and get one of the commis to do it. The thing is, none of the food I loved at Dabbous – the asparagus with the rapeseed oil mayo, the soupy umami-rich squid broth, the slab of barbecued ibérico pork with a sweet-salty toffee mess of praline – was improved because of the tweezer thing. The tweezers were merely used to place edible blooms and micro herbs and tiny shards of this or that which I didn't give a toss about.

In short they were used to garnish. Oh dear, the G word. That is the real problem. The use of tweezers is just a symptom of the garnish disease. Garnishing is the art of the superfluous. It is an expression of prissiness in food, an attempt to make the gloriously knuckle-dragging business of preparing good stuff to eat – put meat on fire, throw fish in frothing butter – look delicate and considered. For here is a universal truth. Nothing classed as a garnish that is sprinkled on to food just before serving is ever necessary. That doesn't include flakes of sea salt or a grind of pepper. That's not garnishing. It's seasoning.

It does include a chiffonade of parsley. Or of basil. Or any other bloody green herb. Have you ever had to do it: chop, chop, chop, turn, scrape together, chop again, until you have both a green dust and lost the will to live? Then you throw it all over the food so that it looks like you placed it right in the path of a Flymo run amok. It doesn't even improve the presentation. Don't believe me? Go get a copy of *Larousse Gastronomique*; not the new 'modernised' version but the old one with all those repellent pictures of food slathered with aspic and roux with the texture of old man sputum. Go look at pictures of pike du

Meunier. Or the pork chops charcutière. Or, frankly, of anything. It's all sprinkled with so much redundant chopped parsley it looks like it's been infected by a virulent mould. You know it will add nothing to the experience of eating the dish.

But perhaps the most shameful crime is the placing of a basil leaf – or 'dessert parsley' as I heard it called recently – on top of a scoop of vanilla ice cream. Especially if placed there with a pair of tweezers. I know it shouldn't make me so cross; that there are worse crimes in the world. I know I should probably get out less. But I can't help myself. Garnishing is the biggest waste of time there is in the kitchen. Take this as a declaration of war.

Where Ingredients Go to Die

For many years in the 1970s my family went on holiday to a Dorset hotel where, on Friday nights, there was a buffet laid out in the dining room. The centrepiece would always be a huge poached salmon, glazed with mayonnaise and decorated with lobster shell appendages for colour and detail, as if the two creatures had met near some radioactive waste outlet and mutated. I remember that salmon very well, and the way a toqued chef stood behind it proudly. I do not recall ever once having eaten it. Even then, with a child's indiscriminate palate and a hog's unceasing appetite, I was suspicious of the way the food was displayed. Could something so played with really taste nice? And were the salads that surrounded it not just last night's leftovers coming around again to say hello?

That suspicion has never left me. As a man who has rarely met a calorie he couldn't hug, I should love a buffet: all that food, fully out there, on display. It is the plunging neckline of gastronomy. Forget the prose interface with the kitchen of a menu. Here is true choice, presented on so much glazed Villeroy & Boch. The problem is that while in principle buffets are a lovely idea, in practice they are where ingredients go to die.

Nobody ever makes a positive choice to mount a buffet; it is a compromise solution to a volume problem. It is the way to feed a hundred at a cheap wedding, where the air is full of regret and disappointment, on quartered pork pies that, after a few hours on the platters, have started to look like the plasticated foods in the windows of dodgy Japanese restaurants. It is curling sandwiches and things on sticks, Scotch eggs the colour of self-tan outside and the mouth-gumming denseness of Sarah Palin within. It is all undressed salad and stale bread and desperation.

Even the ambitious, high-end buffet doesn't do it for me. I have, on occasion, been forced into the American way of Sunday brunch, at those Los Angeles hotels where the women have eyebrows like grave and acute accents. I have stood, flat-footed between the serving stations, studying the cascades of shrimp on ice, and the hunks of beef bleeding into the chopping-board gutters, and the intense and gifted Hispanic men at the omelette hobs begging for orders, and known that nothing good could come from this. The presentation may indeed be beautiful. They may well have recreated Mount Rushmore from fourteen kilos of oyster on the half shell, a pig and a half of glazed tenderloin and a bathtub's worth of Hawaiian tropical fruit. But you know, just know, that the way it looks is as good as this meal is ever going to get. For a start there is always the lingering suspicion, especially on hot Californian days, that one of the beautifully laid out trays is the hidden snub-nosed bullet in a game of edible Russian roulette. Kitchens are great places to keep food. They have fridges and everything. Dining rooms are not. Buffets are a night of vomiting just waiting to happen.

But the main issue is that meals assembled from lists of dishes on menus have, by their nature, a logic. Choices made by reading are intellectualised. You weigh things up against each other, imagine eating them. Meals built from a surfeit of visceral choice, the food stuffed under your nose, have absolutely no logic whatsoever. It's all instinct and dribble, clash and clatter. It is a mayonnaise-drenched salmon with a lobster's head.

Chutney Fever

Autumn arrives, flaunting its abundance, and on my many friends' allotments the branches bend under the weight of their fruit. Accordingly, my front step fills up with gifts. There are supermarket carrier bags stuffed with gnarly apples and pears. There are cardboard boxes overflowing with runner beans or courgettes the size of police truncheons. I look upon this mottled crop with appropriate feelings of gratitude. To my friends and neighbours, I say thank you.

Deep inside me, however, there is something else: a profound sense of inadequacy, a feeling that I am not quite made for these times. Because just what the hell am I supposed to do with it all? Do not for a moment misunderstand me. I am not in any way anti-allotment. I recognise the profound pleasure they give to those who have them. They are a superb educational tool and the work involved is brilliant for both physical fitness and mental well-being.

There's just one problem: all that bloody produce. I know exactly what my response is meant to be. I'm meant to swoon at the orgy of food preserving that lies ahead of me. My heart should go pitter-pitter-pat at all the lacto-fermentation possibilities. Everybody lacto-ferments these days, don't they. You are not a true citizen of the world unless you have developed an intimate relationship with a pulsing, fizzing jar of green matter festering with enough bacterial matter to start a small war.

Instead I want to hide under the duvet until the shameless fecundity has died away. Please don't force me to start sterilising jam jars. Because I'll only end up with serried ranks of chutney I can't use. We've all been there. After an afternoon of boiling and stirring and getting every work surface sticky, you find yourself staring at enough home-made condiment to get you through the siege of Stalingrad. For a couple of weeks you feel virtuous, as if you have served the seasons well. You are mother nature's doula. The process is genuinely fulfilling.

Now you have to eat it all. With smug satisfaction, you start by pairing it with the obvious, things like cheese and cold meats. Look at me, celebrating nature's bounty. Soon you are dropping spoonfuls on the side of hot dishes, as if it was ketchup. Then you start mixing it into stews. Before you know it, you're pouring it on to your cereal or stuffing it down the side of the sofa or smearing it on the cat. Anything to empty the damn jar. Your gaze turns slowly to the shelf. There are another forty-seven jars to go.

So now the un-choreographed dance of the jar exchange begins: here, have some of my beetroot jelly. In return you've brought me some of your courgette jam? How innovative. My, I would never have thought of making kimchi out of broccoli. And so on. It's all so onerous. This is not just my problem. The question most regularly asked on *The Kitchen Cabinet*, BBC Radio 4's food panel show, is about the using up of gluts: of pears or cabbages or leeks. The answer is so often chutney.

I could point out that mass agriculture was invented specifically to avoid these problems. It enables the wide distribution of large-scale production. Again, that would make me sound like I'm down on the grow-your-own thing and I'm really not. But it does have consequences, namely the tyranny of the glut, and I don't have the stomach for it. There's only one solution. I'm going back to bed. Wake me when autumn is over.

Moved to Tears

Welcome to gastronomic hell. Or, to be more exact, seat 24, carriage C, on the 11 a.m. to Bristol Temple Meads. For it is autumn and I am travelling again, from one end of the United Kingdom to the other. There will be planes, trains and automobiles and while punctuality can't be guaranteed, one thing is certain: the eating options will be truly awful. We like to think we have gone through a food revolution in this country over the past few decades and in terms of restaurants, and availability of ingredients, we have. But start travelling by public transport or, God help you, pull into a motorway services, and it becomes clear that revolution is still at the Molotov cocktail-throwing stage.

In Bristol or Peckham or Ancoats right now it's all 'nduja and seared hispi cabbage and roasted golden beetroot with whipped feta. Meanwhile on the 11 a.m. to Temple Meads it's 'Would you like to avail yourself of our coffee and Twix deal for £3?' and 'Just how bad would you like to feel about yourself today?' The fact is you can have anything you like when you're on the move in Britain as long as it's a bolus of oil-drenched carbs. There are sugar-spiked muffins, and dismal croissants so flaccid no form of culinary Viagra would ever get them up again. The buffet car sandwiches taste of profit margin and old age. The 'healthy option' on board is a bag of salted peanuts. Get on a domestic flight and a mini-tube of paprika-flavour Pringles is about as close as you'll get to an act of self-care. And in a well-equipped motor-way services you'll have the full choice from Burger King to KFC to Costa.

Try to deal with the problem and people will point and laugh. An example: *The Kitchen Cabinet*, the food panel show I present for BBC Radio 4, generally gets to and from the locations of our early evening live records by train. At the end, those of us heading back to London get on board, fully aware that the choice in the buffet car was appalling in the morning and now, gone 8 p.m., will be a meagre choice of awful. So we have a train picnic purchased in advance: olives and charcuterie, hummus and good cheeses and fresh fruit. One evening I posted a picture of this to Twitter, as we hurtled back from Birmingham or Stoke or Stafford.

It was such an extraordinary sight, this train table of nice things to eat, that hundreds of people piled in with their comments. Which in turn result-ed in MailOnline running a story about how I had divided Twitter with my 'VERY middle-class train picnic'. There were reasonable complaints about the amount of plastic. Some questioned the etiquette around eating possibly stinky foods in an open carriage. Taramasalata and sourdough crackers, anyone? Honestly, the *Kitchen Cabinet* team would happily avoid both of these issues if our train had boasted the kind of modestly ambitious dining car of the sort other countries' rail operators seem to manage. But almost all of them have been phased out in the UK.

Instead we have little choice but to raid the nearest Waitrose for the cream of their 'Essentials' range. From time to time, just as with hospital food, there is an initiative. A well-known, well-meaning chef is hired to put his name to a range of products on board a train. The branding is always gorgeous. But the contents amount to the same thing: carb on carb on carb. Perhaps you disagree. If so, you are welcome to come and argue the point. You'll find me in a sugar-induced coma in coach C.

OUT TO LUNCH

People Watching

A Sunday lunchtime in the eternal spring sunshine of a Los Angeles autumn and I have a table for one at the venerable Nate 'n Al's delicatessen. It's a reminder that the film industry was founded by Ashkenazi Jews from the east coast who craved a taste of home: of pastrami on rye and matzo ball soup, food for colder weather and darker skies but to hell with that. If this is what these film people want to eat this is what they'll have. After all they write the script.

And here it is seventy years on, still doing the same thing it has always done. I am at Nate 'n Al's for the smoked salmon and the 'everything' bagel, but for something else too: the people watching. The pleasures of eating alone are obvious. You get to eat what you want, how you want. It is one of adulthood's great indulgences. But who admits to its other profound pleasure, the licence it gives you to spy on people?

We reveal so very much of ourselves at the table. It is a vital bodily function we perform in public. Witness the man who carefully lifts the crisped skin off his roast chicken, pushing it to the side of his plate with disgust, or the woman who, faced by spare ribs, sets to work with a knife and fork. We immediately feel we know something about both of them, none of it attractive.

And even if we can't be sure of their stories, we can quietly invent them. In the booth next to mine at Nate 'n Al's today is a young father with his small daughter filling in her colouring book. So he's a divorced dad, and it's his Sunday to take her out. No, hang on. Because here comes his wife with their younger child. But she attends only to the kids and the couple barely exchange glances. He pulls the wedding ring off the appropriate finger and puts it back on again, repeatedly, like it's something he's done many times. So no, not a divorced dad's Sunday. At least, not quite yet.

On the other side of the aisle, there's a party of three in their late sixties. A couple on one side of the table, a single man on the other. Once upon a time surely they were four? But she is no longer here, and they make a point to look after him as she would have wanted. So on a Sunday they are still at Nate 'n Al's because certain traditions need observing.

Just in front of me, a Jewish mamma is issuing instructions to the long-suffering waitress as if the Meg Ryan diner scenes in *When Harry Met Sally* were less social satire than a guide for living. She wants the onions on one plate, and make sure they don't burn the bagel, because haven't you heard that burnt toast gives you cancer and God forbid the oncologists of Beverly Hills should get more business?

And perhaps way over on the other side, out of my view, is a woman eating alone. Perhaps she looks up from her plate and sees a big man with too much hair and a beard. She watches the way he stares around the room and thinks, 'Poor sap, deep in his midlife crisis,' and returns to her lunch. Is she right? Has she nailed it? That's not for me to say. For the duration of lunch the solo diner gets to own these narratives. Because without them, eating alone would just be nowhere near as fun.

A Terrible Inconvenience

I am standing in the basement of a restaurant, feeling the fear. Before me are two doors, marked with logos. One is a circle with a crossed line pointing down; the other, a circle with an arrow pointing off to the right. Of course, I should be able to tell which is which. But down here in the gloom, I am uncertain. I look at my phone, anxiously. Naturally there's no signal down here. I can't check.

All I want is a pee. But I stand now on the threshold of an incident. Choose the wrong logo – the wrong door – and I'll be the perv who barged into the ladies' loo. I don't want to be that perv. Suddenly a woman comes out of the door marked by the circle with the down cross. I grin at her gratefully. She looks at me as if, at the very least, I'm a candidate for suspicion. I rush off through the other door. Relief.

There are myriad ways by which restaurants complicate things. We know what they are: non-plate serving items, menus with print so small you need a torch to read it by, waiters taking orders without notebooks and so on. But there should be a special place reserved in hell for those that, in a desperate effort to look smart or interesting, manage to complicate the simple business of using the loo mid-meal by using whacky or, worse, completely indecipherable markings on toilet doors.

Anything – anything at all – which makes you pause, even just out of irritation, should be punishable by a massive fine, or at the very least extreme tutting. It starts with the most simplistic of pictograms, the ones that are so familiar we barely notice them any more, by which I mean those that insist women are instantly recognisable because they always wear skirts. (I'm rather taken by the oppositional re-engineering of that image online, which shows it was actually a superhero's cape all along.) Then the silliness begins. At Star Inn the City in York – a place with form; they used to serve bread in flat caps – the doors are marked 'Olafs' and 'Helgas', presumably because of the city's Viking heritage or because the management hates its customers. Really! Stop it! Stop it now!

At the venerable River Café the men's toilets are defined as such by being blue. The women's are obviously, therefore, pink. A ballpoint pen manufacturer pulls that kind of stunt, and social media explodes. There are so many more: the Japanese places that mark them 'samurai' and 'geisha', which manages the neat trick of being annoying, a cultural stereotype and misogynist all at the same time; the gastro pub which marks them 'dolls' and 'pistols'; the seafood restaurant that marks them 'gulls' and 'buoys', which barely makes sense. And then there are all the graphic ones, giving topographical views of genitalia. God help us.

Apart from the fact that these are all the worst ideas from Planet Stupid, there's another concern: that women will become as confused as I was, inadvertently walk into the men's and discover the dreadful truth. All men's toilets are disgusting. Men have issues with aim. It's tragic but it's true.

The solution is obvious and, happily, already being adopted by some. We don't have gender-defined toilets at home so why have them in restaurants? Scrap the word 'men'. Get rid of the word 'women'. Just give us a bunch of cubicles marked 'toilet'. It will do the job. What's more it will save me both from the fear and, rather importantly, extreme embarrassment.

Hell Is Other People

As Jean-Paul Sartre once wrote, hell is other people. Many would agree, including the London-based Russian restaurateur Arkady Novikov. Recently he used an interview to slag off a whole bunch of hellish people, namely spendy Russians. 'I find it embarrassing,' he said. 'Who are these girls drinking champagne and carrying crocodile Birkin bags? It's like a disease people get when they have money. I don't want to be associated with this thing.' Doesn't he? That's unfortunate because, as he acknowledges, they are precisely the ones thronging the £100-a-head gastro-disaster that is Novikov in London's Mayfair. If you haven't heard of Novikov be grateful. It's Dante's forty-sixth circle of hell, a nose-bleedingly expensive septic tank containing all that is wrong with flash restaurants, where the Italian food tastes like cheap Chinese and the Imperial sashimi platter costs £227. Before service.

Dear old Arkady is at liberty to slag off Russians in London. I am not. Instead I will simply slag off everybody with stupid money, whichever corner of the globe they happen to come from, including our own. God knows there's enough of them. Right now there's a luxe food economy, focused on a couple of London postcodes, which is entirely supported by a grotesque, preening, Louboutin-heeled, gold-plated iPhone-carrying, plastic-crashing, Bugatti-driving, natural resource-pillaging, tax-dodging excuse for humanity that floats like some gold-flecked scummy head on the warm beer of the rest of an economy simply trying to make do.

There has been a massive explosion in high-end restaurants in recent years. None of them would exist were it not for this lot, a species apart, which simply adores London's tax-friendly accountancy rules. They sit nightly at the tables, flicking selfies at each other on digital currents, air-kissing one another's bottle-bronzed cheeks, their botoxed eyebrows feigning constant surprise, while picking irritably at platters of exquisitely carved Jamón Ibérico, or Peking duck with skin like lacquered rosewood, or bits of sashimi cut just so.

For this is the real tragedy. Novikov may be a clearing house for lumps of killer protein destined only to be tortured into submission. But many of these restaurants are actually rather good: superb ingredients, great cooking, skilled service. And all of it is completely wasted on the very people who can afford it; the ones who book into them not out of greed or even a tinge of hunger, but because they like the way the lighting flatters their complexion and the toiletries in the bogs make them smell like one of Dita Von Teese's freshly pampered armpits.

It gets worse. Obviously there are people who don't give a toss about restaurants like this. Even if they were in a position to save up, this is not how they would wish to spend their money. Fair enough. But there are many others who do care, who will strain to save the necessary pile of cash needed for their one high end eating-out event of the year, only to find themselves locked in a dining room with a Premiership-quality bunch of tossers. What's more, as we now know, were it not for all the people those expensive restaurants are wasted upon, they wouldn't even be in business for the people who do appreciate them. Of course some of you may have clocked that I don't just go to them once a year. I have to go all the time. And finally you recognise the depth of my tragedy. Being a restaurant critic is assumed to be heaven. It's meant to be bliss. Instead, because of other people, it all too often becomes something else: a complete and utter hell.

Stop the Clock

How long does it take you to eat your dinner? By which I mean a proper dinner: three courses; elbows on the table; yes, I'd love a coffee; now finish your anecdote? I only ask because, increasingly, certain restaurants think there's a strong chance that instead of coming to eat some lovely food and have a jolly time, you might be intent on table blocking. They are instituting time limits. At places like Novikov and Sushisamba, Aqua Shard and so many more, restaurants where the prices will make your credit card smell of burning plastic, you are told the table is yours for two hours and no more. Clear off. Charmed, I'm sure.

This peaked with one opening – they'll remain nameless to protect the guilty – which said you might have to give your table back after ninety minutes. This is a restaurant where three courses, with a cheaper bottle of wine, will cost £60 a head or 66p a minute. I suggested via Twitter that this was a bit much. They were indignant. They told me they were a lovely, relaxed restaurant but that some people might want to have a quicker meal before the theatre.

In which case the diner will surely be the one to tell you they need to be out quickly. Here's what I don't understand. Restaurants are in charge of their own service. Either they know how long it takes them to serve a full meal or they don't. If they can get it done within ninety minutes or two hours they don't need to institute a time limit. And if they can't, then the time limit is useless. Is lingering over the petits fours now a crime?

Let's not pretend. My ludicrous job as a restaurant critic, with its greasy patina of assumed entitlement, means I'm unlikely ever to be told to get off my table. But I do remember the acute anxiety I felt the first time I came across a two-hour time limit at Yauatcha a few years back. I sat there worrying whether their failure to take my order for twenty minutes was part of the tick, tick, tick. After that, was I eating fast enough? I assumed it was a bizarre one-off. How wrong I was.

Why has this happened? Partly it's the increasingly brutal economics of the restaurant business. To make a profit they have to turn tables and they want to make doing so easier. But I think a major part has been played by technology, which is to say, online booking systems. Obviously, yay technology! We all love being able to plan our evening via a few clicks. But it does make it easier to add small print online making outrageous demands that few reasonable people could ever bring themselves to mention if they were talking to the customer over the phone. (The most outrageous example: the £5 charge for a window seat at the Marco Pierre White Steakhouse in Birmingham. I adore Birmingham, but I'm not paying a fiver to look at it.)

It's just not very hospitable, which is a crying shame for the hospitality business. Plus, it can work both ways. I suspect one reason there's been a rise in no-shows is people feeling less beholden to a booking because they did it online rather than by talking to a human being. That's not to excuse the behaviour; it's just an unintended consequence. It's something I fully intend to discuss with my friends in detail the next time I go out for dinner. If they allow me enough time.

Thanks for the Memories

Not long ago I went out for dinner. And that's all I can tell you. Except that the restaurant was in Hoxton. Or Peckham. Though it may have been in Carlisle. Anyway, there was short rib. Definitely short rib. Or perhaps hanger steak. Or chicken. Nah, I've got nothing for you. The whole meal is a black hole. My time went in and absolutely nothing came out.

Some eating experiences are like that. When I started as a restaurant critic I used to take notes. The fish was soft. The chips were crisp. The raspberries were sweet. I would write these words down studiously, page after page, with a plan to come up with better ones when I wrote the review. Until one day I forgot my notebook and realised I hadn't ever needed one. Either a dish was memorable and therefore I could write about it, or my mind was a complete blank, and I could write about that instead.

It's common these days to point and laugh at restaurants which do stupid things to their food to make it memorable: the ones who serve their dishes in mini wheelbarrows or hollowed-out sheep skulls or on slates, and I am very happy to join in with this. I love a roaring mob, me. But what's most curious about all that stuff is it's wasted effort. Those stupid food service items are bound to fail. Sure, we'll all remember the mini wheelbarrow or the sheep's skull, but we're never going to remember the food that was actually in it. The things that make food memorable are never about the accessories. They are so much more subtle, so much more emotional than that.

When, as a small child, I was ill, my mother would make me boiled eggs mushed up with warm pieces of buttered toast. It was basically boiled eggs and soldiers without all the admin. I can still remember the texture; the way the soft, slippery yolks rubbed up against the crisped toast. Even today, buttery eggs make me think of the hotness of the bed sheets and the tone of my mother's voice, though not the words.

In adulthood I have other memories. I recall an open shellfish lasagne eaten at the wonderful Champignon Sauvage in Cheltenham in the early nineties, before few had heard of either it or chef David Everitt-Matthias. It was the first meal of ambition I had paid for with my own money and that pride, at a kind of adulthood obtained, only emphasised the intensity of the boisterous flavours. Eating oysters at the ramshackle Company Shed in West Mersea in Essex, where the water and land negotiate endlessly with each other, I tasted the brine and slap of the sea and felt like I was somewhere far off the edge of my known world. A breakfast of pancakes and maple syrup eaten in a diner on West 44th, on my first ever morning in New York, will never be forgotten. The pancakes weren't particularly special, but the breakfast seriously was.

Do I need to tell you that the shellfish lasagne would not have been more memorable if it had been served to me in a mini wheelbarrow? That those oysters were going to stay with me for life without being presented on a ship's anchor? No, I thought not. And that's the point. While chefs are busy trying to manufacture the 'wow' factor, we are there supplying our own. Chefs can try as hard as they like. They can raid roofs for their slates. But I'm afraid it just won't make it happen.

What Are Restaurants Good For?

Journalists are paid to report what they see, and as a result they get to see terrible things. Being a restaurant critic, I know far too much about this. Oh, the atrocities I have witnessed. The most recent was at the Birnam Brasserie inside the Gleneagles Hotel. They called it a cassoulet. I would call it the death of all that is good and hopeful in the world. The problem with that so-called 'cassoulet' – I'm using those quotation marks like weapons – was not just a bad day in the kitchen. It's a systemic issue to do with the way restaurant kitchens work; one that means there are many dishes which should be left entirely to the home cook and never ordered from a menu.

Restaurant kitchens like to break dishes down to their constituent parts, only to be assembled when an order arrives. In theory this enables quality control over each element and saves on wastage. A cassoulet should be a concoction in which all the elements spend twenty-four hours getting to know each other. But if too few people order such a finished, melded dish it can't be recycled. If the various ingredients are kept apart until the last moment they can have an alternative future. And so instead of receiving a cassoulet you get violated beans with some pig bits plonked on top.

For the same reason, if you order a crumble you won't get a crumble. You'll get everything you deserve, which is to say some pre-stewed fruit, with biscuit rubble plonked on top, and a dismal sense of misery at what could have been had you stayed home and made your own damn crumble. It's why restaurant kitchens infuriate the pie liberationists by sending out stew with a plank of pastry on top. If you want a pie make it at home. Or get a takeaway from Greggs. They sell enough baked goods to do them properly.

Restaurants are also terrible at anything which takes time. My roast potatoes are better than every roast potato I have ever been served in a restaurant. Mine are crunchier, richer and ruder than any professional's. My Yorkshire puddings are better. And then there's roast chicken. I've eaten many of the big marquee names of the roast chicken world: the poulet de Bresse at Chez L'Ami Louis in Paris, at time of writing yours for €95+. There's the famed chicken at Zuni Café in San Francisco, which I feel no need to ever eat again, and the black leg chicken at La Petite Maison in London, which I now can't afford. When the latter opened in 2007 it cost £35. Now it's £105, which just makes me want to stick drawing pins in my forehead so I think about something else. Plus, the one I do at home is always better and I'll fight anyone who argues.

Restaurant kitchens screw up cheese on toast. It's too simple and they don't know what to do with simple. Scrambled eggs baffle them, and while macaroni cheese may now be a thing, it's nowhere near as good a thing eaten out as it is eaten in my house. The tragedy is that I keep ordering all this stuff, my soul deep-basted in hope. This time, I think. This time it will be good. But it never is. Don't get me wrong. Restaurant kitchens are brilliant at many, many things. I depend on them to be so. But when it comes to the comforting, it all falls apart. Chefs are stumped by the homely. Which is why that's where those dishes should stay: at home.

JINGLE ALL THE WAY

My Christmas Food Commandments

For boring technical reasons to do with him predating the birth of Jesus by about thirteen centuries, and being really quite Jewish, Moses was never in a position to lay down the law where Christmas is concerned. This strikes me as a terrible omission because God knows we could all do with the help. But do not fear. I feel uniquely placed to take on the mantle of dear Moses and have a crack at a bunch of commandments for Christmas. You can ignore them if you like, but on your own head be it.

One: thou shalt not mistake Nigella, Mary and Jamie for the Lord, thy God. Those Christmas specials are only television programmes. They're entertainment, not a blueprint for how your Christmas is meant to be. Yours won't be anything like that because you don't have battalions of home economists to knock up the food and set designers to decorate the house. Even Nigella's won't be like that. Two: thou shalt not always make thine own. There is no shame in buying ready-made bread sauce or mince pies. That's why supermarket New Product Development units were invented. Three: if you're the cook on Christmas

Day, thou shalt have first crack at the sausages and bacon as they come out of the oven.

Four: thou shalt not feel compelled to make every side dish ever invented. Roast potatoes, and one other vegetable, two at a push. No more. What are you trying to prove? That you're a whizz at Oven Tetris? No one will judge you. As long as there's gravy everything will be fine. (This last rule applies all year round.) Five: thou shalt not wear a stupid hat during lunch if thou doesn't want to. Even if the children whine at you for being a spoilsport. Children need to learn that one of the pleasures of adulthood is not having to do stupid things.

Six: thou shalt not serve Christmas pudding, at least not on Christmas Day. Nobody likes it. And even if they do, by the time you get to dessert at Christmas lunch nobody has any space. All they want is jelly. Make jelly and if anyone complains, tell them Moses made you. If you must serve Christmas pudding, wait until the week between Christmas and New Year, buy it up cheap, steam it, then fry it in bacon fat. You'll thank me. I'm a biblical prophet; I know what I'm talking about.

Seven: thou shalt eat trifle for breakfast on Boxing Day. It's Christmas. The usual rules do not apply. Eight: thou shalt not be embarrassed about making exactly the same things from leftovers as always. Yes, we all know your turkey curry is awful. It's always been awful. But tradition is important and your awful turkey curry is one of them. Stop trying to reinvent the wheel. Though don't make that turkey risotto thing with the frozen peas again. That really is a crime against food.

Nine: thou shalt drink Baileys, though only at this time of year. Drinking it at any other time of year marks you out as having the palate of a seven-year-old. Drinking it at Christmas defines you as sweet and sentimental. And finally, ten: thou shalt have a meltdown if thou wants to. In theory, Christmas is a delightful festival, a time to draw near to your loved ones. In practice it's a bloody nightmare, a breeding ground for recrimination and, eventually, divorce. Far better to get it all out there. Other than that, it's peace and goodwill all the way. Merry Christmas everyone. And you're welcome.

How to Avoid Christmas

Like your first hangover and your first speeding ticket, cooking Christmas lunch for the first time is a rite of passage. It is a passing of the flame from one generation to the next, with added gravy. I remember mine as if it was twenty-five years ago. Two things stay with me. One was my mother's nod of approval at the sweet and sour red cabbage. It wasn't her red cabbage. It could never be hers. But it did deserve to be eaten. That was praise enough.

The other memory was the admin. Blimey, it was complicated. I had to write timetables, like I was revising for A Levels all over again, only with a greater risk of humiliation through failure. Pinned down by the fridge magnets were documents that had taken on the significance of holy scripture: '12 noon – potatoes in; 1.30 p.m., bird out'. And so on. When it was all done and the kitchen was festooned in edible wreckage, I took the applause and muttered quietly about not making a habit of it.

And yet, come year two I was in the kitchen again, right up to my wrist in the turkey. It was the same the next year and the year after that. For somewhere along the way, I had made a quiet but astonishing discovery, one that most Christmas Day cooks will recognise but never acknowledge. They don't want to be found out, because intriguingly it goes against the very spirit of Christmas itself. It is this: cooking Christmas lunch is a glorious way to absent yourself from the nightmare of Christmas; from the weird, twisted dynamic of one long day crammed together with your family.

It's perfect. There has to be a Christmas lunch. Whoever cooks it is seen as performing a selfless service. Look at them toiling over the sprouts and the parsnips and the roasties and the pigs in blankets and no really, I'm fine, you go back in there and relax. I've got this. If you are up to the job, spending the first few hours of the day locked in the kitchen can be much more pleasurable than tolerating your racist auntie. Plus, courtesy of natural justice, you get let off the washing up. It is a big, hearty bundle of wins.

It took me a while to clock that my mother had pulled this trick throughout my childhood. She hated her own in-laws but also knew they had to be there. She had a two-pronged approach to the problem. The first was to invite an enormous number of people. Christmas Day in our house could have up to thirty people at the table, mostly gay men, Jews and actors: gay men because in the seventies, sadly, many of them had mislaid their families; Jews because they weren't really meant to be marking the pagan feast at all so were always free; and actors because they were caught between performances of panto on Christmas Eve and Boxing Day and couldn't get back to their own families. Many of them were gay Jewish actors.

Having hidden my paternal grandparents in this relentlessly jazz-hands crowd, she then disappeared into the kitchen, guaranteeing she was as far away from them as possible. Now I've described this, of course, the game is up. So here's what you do. This year, come the big day, don't let them get away with it. Everybody should set up camp in the kitchen, telling the self-absenting cook that you don't want them to feel left out. It will drive them completely nuts. Merry Christmas.

The Christmas Meat Sweats

I have the meat sweats. The Christmas meat sweats. I know what you're thinking: it's too early for this kind of thing; trust me, it isn't. This is exactly when they strike, six weeks out from the big day. You wake in the night, and a restless mind searching for a route back to unconsciousness gets prodded by just one question: which animal are you going to cook on Christmas Day?

In the 1970s, when I was a kid, it was so simple. You had turkey. Nobody actually liked it, but then there were loads of things in the 1970s we didn't like but put up with: beds with sheets and blankets, instant mashed potato, *Terry and June*. Intensively reared, brutally tough, tasteless turkey with breast meat the colour of a healing knife wound was just something we had to endure. We were all in it together. At least there was enough meat to feed all those family members we hated but were forced to sit down with.

Now, of course, if you choose turkey, you have to justify it by storing up enough information for a pack of Top Trumps cards. 'Well of course, a turkey is actually a game bird, so . . .' So what, exactly? We should shoot it? Game bird it might once have been but it long ago forgot how to run away. You have to use the word 'Bronze' attached to its location. It's from Suffolk or Norfolk or some mythical Turkey Shangri-La off the A120 near Braintree. Follow that up with a long speech about how you need to roast it fast or slow or brine it first or just drop the whole damn thing in the deep fat fryer 'because that's how they do it in the American south'. Which is not a recommendation; there are loads of things they do in the American south that you shouldn't, because many are regarded as risky behaviour by the health authorities.

So instead you announce you're going to do a rib of beef, 'because traditionally that was what was served on the British table on Christmas Day'. Except now everyone looks at you like you think it's just another Sunday lunch and you have entirely missed the point. Okay then, goose. What about goose? Very festive, goose. Don't get me started. Have you tried roasting one of those? Within an hour there is a thick film of grease across every surface in your kitchen, as if you were planning to stage all-in slippery wrestling bouts there as post-lunch entertainment. What's more, they're seriously expensive and have almost no meat on them. Gosh, goose! Delicious! Is there any more? No. No there isn't. Shut up and have another potato.

That leaves you with the three-bird roast. Very expensive, of course: the doddery peers of the House of Lords love three-bird roasts. But there's more than enough to go around, and it cooks relatively quickly. The only problem is cosmetic. Merry Christmas everyone. This year I've cooked you . . . a loaf of bread. That's what a three-bird roast looks like, a big block of something knocked up by an artisanal baker with a surfeit of wholegrain. You don't know whether to carve it or toast it. No, Christmas demands something impressive. Which means you're back to the big-titted turkey.

And still sleep evades you. But I've solved the problem. I'm dodging it altogether. This year, to keep things really special, my lot are having Findus Crispy Pancakes and Angel Delight. Job done. Now then, who's coming round mine for Christmas Day?

Christmas Smells

It was the smell of Elnett that did it to me. One moment I was a fifty-something man. The next, I was a four-year-old boy again. It was just before the start of one of my live shows and I was in the dressing room, staring at myself in the mirror. I concluded my never less than ludicrous hair looked tonight like it had been styled courtesy of me stuffing my wet fingers into a plug socket. Something had to be done. Which was when I spotted the can of Elnett, left behind by a previous performer. I damped down my so-called hairstyle, and went to work setting it in place.

The intensity of the smell of the hair lacquer took me by surprise. It was bitter and acrid in a way which caught at the back of the throat, but also heavily perfumed, as though trying to hide its true industrial nature. It was the smell of my mother, just before she went out for the night; it was the smell of the adult world, of glamour and also of something else. Abandonment would be too strong a word for it, but certainly disappointment would do the job. I was once again the small child standing in my parents' room watching and smelling the finishing touches being put in place, before she left me to the casual indifference of the babysitter.

It's fitting that it should have happened at this time of year because, frankly, Christmas stinks. There is no other time of the year so completely enveloped by smells. It is wistfulness in three dimensions which, as winter darkness closes in, transports us. We gasp and sigh at the twinkly lights. We find a place in our souls for kitsch. But it's the seasonal smells which really hammer away. Certainly, they hammer away at me. Awakened by the olfactory punch of Elnett, I have become like Jean-Baptiste Grenouille, the found-ling anti-hero of Patrick Süskind's magnificent novel *Perfume*, who navigates his way through eighteenth-century French society courtesy of a talent for identi-fying aromas.

These are the weeks of clove and cinnamon, of gin-ger and booze-soaked fruit. It's not universally pleas-ant. The right mix of spices can take me to the cheery thought of a boiling pot of wine, mulled because throwing dried bits of tree bark into substandard wine we wouldn't dare touch at any other time of year makes a twisted kind of sense. But if the scent of cinnamon is too artificial, too much like something engineered to mask the smell of the human in a public toilet, suddenly I am wafted to the lobby of a high-end hotel in Dubai. It is the weeks just before Christmas a

109

decade ago, and I am assailed by the memory of feeling so very out of place and so terribly far from home.

There is science to explain all this. Apparently, the part of our brain which recognises smells also stores our emotional responses. It's designed this way to tell us whether what we are smelling is something we need be scared of or not. It's useful to know how it works, but that doesn't describe the personal impact of smelling, say, the virtuous interplay of smoked, cured pig and its clove-studded treacle glaze, in the moments before the ham leaves the oven. It doesn't describe the hit of dried sage used in a stuffing, or the sickly sweetness inside a tin of Quality Street when you prise the lid off. Indeed, I've come to the conclusion that Christmas really isn't about family, or presents, or food. It's all about the smells. Now do excuse me. I've got to go and snort some more hairspray.

The End of Civilisation as We Know It

There is no deathlier phrase in the world of food than 'It's just a bit of fun.' Something being just a bit of fun is what leads from the gateway drug of a steak served on a slate so that cutting up your dinner sounds like fingernails being dragged down a blackboard, to a full English breakfast served in a dog-food bowl, to a spare rib selection presented in a mini galvanised dustbin.

Just a bit of fun is the excuse for a record-breaking hamburger weighing more than a metric ton, which no one wants to eat; for a $169 hot dog topped with caviar and truffles, which sounds disgusting; for a £130 Wagyu sandwich, which really isn't all that. It's not fun. It's seriously bloody annoying. What's more, it may well be a harbinger for the end of everything we hold dear. And as each Christmas approaches, the volume of this nightmarish stuff only increases.

In 1976, the gloriously named General Sir John Glubb, a distinguished soldier and scholar, wrote a celebrated essay examining how apparently impregnable empires collapse. An age of enterprise leads in turn to an age of affluence, he said, followed inexorably by the age of decadence. In these, the death throes of once great civilisations, the chimera of happiness is pursued through conspicuous consumption, especially involving food and drink. Feasting and boozing was, for example, a particular feature of the Roman Empire before it fell apart.

To witness history repeating itself, I once visited a branch of John Lewis where, for the festive season, they had installed the Kit Kat Chocolatory. It invited you to commission your own bespoke Kit Kat from a bunch of fillings, toppings and chocolates giving up to 1,500 permutations. But the one they really wanted me to perv over was the limited-edition gold Kit Kat, a raspberry and pomegranate-flavoured number covered with twenty-three-carat gold leaf. It cost £25. For a Kit Kat. And no, I didn't try it. I am a man of principle.

Elsewhere, a winter food festival announced the creation of a single pig in a blanket the height of Dwayne 'The Rock' Johnson. It was wrapped in enough bacon to make a wardrobe full of meat ball gowns for Lady Gaga. And then there was the press release I received, breathlessly asking me whether what they had created could possibly be 'the most expensive Panettone in the world'? As if that was something we'd all been waiting for. I shall not name the company responsible. That's exactly what they wanted me to do and I refuse to be played.

It cost £200, a price achieved not through the use of gorgeous ingredients, for there really is nothing worth baking into a sweet, sultana-studded enriched loaf of bread which could get it to such lofty heights. The only way they had been able to get to that price is, of course, by covering the damn thing in, yes, you guessed it, gold leaf: a precious metal which will only pass through you, and turn your bodily product into something sparkly you might briefly consider hanging on the Christmas tree.

We have a saying in journalism. One is an example. Two is a coincidence. But three? That's a trend, and it's very hard to ignore this one. The very least you can say is that there are a bunch of catastrophically unimaginative, dismally uncreative PR and marketing executives who think this obscene 'bit of fun' is the way to make a splash. I think it's something else. I think it's proof that we really are all going to hell in a handcart. And it's various people in the food world who are pulling the damn thing.

FOOD FOR THOUGHT

He's Leaving Home

If I want to understand the profound change my family has undergone I need only look in the fridge. For in there, piled one atop the other, I will find them: Tupperware boxes, stuffed full of leftovers. Obviously, leftovers in our fridge are nothing new. What's changed is the volume of them. The fact is our eldest child has left home for university, and while I feel his absence in the lack of discarded clothes on the floor of his room and the silencing of the banter guns, when I get to the stove, I simply forget: I cook as if we were still four, not three. I suffer an abject failure of portion control.

The amount we cook is much more than a matter of mere practicalities. It is an expression of self, of history. Doubtless, there are those who will now wish to indulge in a bout of furious virtue signalling by pointing out the existence of food banks, and of those just scraping by. This portion size failure of mine is clearly the worst kind of over-privilege. Well, yes. Of course. But doubtless, the complainers didn't grow up with a mother who knew genuine food poverty; a woman who, as an evacuee, recalled stealing swedes from a farmer's field to supplement her diet. For her, the act of over-catering was not just a mark of generosity. It was a way of declaring victory over the odds that had been stacked against her.

As a kid I picked up on all of that, but on other things too: a sense of preparedness, for who knew who might be coming through the door at any moment, in need of feeding? Granted, pogroms weren't a big part of North Wembley life in the 1970s, but cultural memories run deep. Perhaps too it was a way for my mother to express the maternal love that her own feckless mother had been so very short on. The end result was the same. It was a heaving table, a place of 'seconds' and 'clean the plate' and 'more' and I took that to be normal. You didn't really think this sizable arse of mine built itself, did you? As a kid I would eat at friends' homes – let's not pretend; usually non-Jewish friends' homes – and find myself baffled by the culture of 'one each and no more'. You mean you don't do seconds? Oh. There were clearly two types of family and I knew exactly which I came from.

Then I became a parent, and the instinct to provide kicked in. It was my job to fill the table, and I did it according to the only model I knew. A second child arrived, and then all their friends, so each evening you weren't sure how many you would be feeding until you did a headcount.

The years pass, along with A Levels, and suddenly you're buying them their own wok and waving them off. You remain at home fretting about whether they are feeding themselves. You do this worrying as you stir the overfilled pot each night, oblivious to the fact that it contains too much. Until everyone has been served, and you are reaching once more for the Tupperware. The excess doesn't go to waste. Weekday lunches at home are just of a better quality than once they were. And in time, I'll learn to cook for three, not four. But I can't pretend. Restraint just isn't a skill I ever really wanted to acquire. I don't ever want to be the person who cooks only enough.

Pass It On

Recently on *The Kitchen Cabinet*, the panel was asked what dishes they had inherited from their parents. There was sweet talk of dense stews and shepherd's pies. As the chair of the show I didn't need to answer and I was grateful for the fact. As disloyal as it sounds, I didn't have much to say. There's a salad I make – lots of thinly sliced peppers, red onions, torn basil – which I picked up from my mother, but I think she got it out of Craig Claiborne's *New York Times Cookbook*. Other than that, while my mother was a good cook, she was very much of her time. I have no desire to make the utter faff that is coulibiac (salmon, wild rice and boiled eggs in a puff pastry shell; her go-to show-off dinner party dish) and I will not torture my kids with spaghetti marrow as she once tortured me.

I suspect I am not alone. We may inherit an interest in the table from our parents but not the dishes themselves. In this there are many who think wistfully that we have lost something, which is to misunderstand what the passing on of recipes and methods was all about. The key inherited dishes of Britain, the sort documented by the social historian Dorothy Hartley in her book *Food in England*, were inherited by necessity rather than a sentimental attachment to tradition or 'the old ways'.

You grew up in the village where you would die. You learnt how to deal with the whole of the pig when it came to slaughter time so it would last through the year. You learnt how to make one kind of bread from the newly ground flour and a different kind of bread from the same flour six months later when it had taken on different qualities. You might look to the distant hills and wonder what was over the other side, but you were unlikely to go there.

Now we are mobile in so many ways. We cross those hills and keep on going, and are spared the worry of the flour's ageing. While the sentimental will mourn the passing of a certain community cohesion, the reality is that social immobility was a function of poverty. You didn't go anywhere else because you couldn't afford to. So you stayed home and cured pork belly for bacon like your mother and her mother before her.

Now generally if we cook our parents' food it is to take us to an emotional place rather than a gastronomic one. Otherwise we cook freely and vividly as our curiosities take us, and that has to be a good thing. Of course it makes the idea of passing on recipes more than ludicrous: 'My son, I bequeath to you this recipe for chargrilled chicken wings with a miso glaze and kimchi slaw which has been in our family for, oooh, eighteen months now, since Uncle Derek gave me that modern Korean cookbook the Christmas before last.' No, perhaps not.

What does that leave us parents with? In terms of actual recipes, not much. In time even modern classics like the River Café cookbooks or Nigella's *How to Eat* will age and date. Our kids will laugh and roll their eyes. Instead we bequeath to our sons and daughters an enthusiasm for food and a sense of adventure. We pass on self-reliance and knife skills, and a smear of good taste, the weird, dated bits of which they will rightly discard. Then we cross our fingers and hope for an invitation to dinner.

Make Lunch Not War

Recently, I fell into an email correspondence with a Bosnian writer and stand-up comedian called Mirko Bozic. We were discussing one of my less positive restaurant reviews. It seems the appetite for a scathing takedown is just as pronounced in the Balkans as it is in London. His analysis of what made for good food was fun, but it was when he told me that he was writing from Mostar that I leaned into my computer screen.

Back in the early nineties, I worked on a newspaper feature about the Stari Most, the gorgeous sixteenth-century Ottoman bridge that crossed the Neretva river, linking the city's various communities. In November 1993, at the height of the brutal Bosnian war, the bridge was destroyed. Of course, it was a horrendous piece of cultural vandalism. But it was also a blunt, physical symbol for what was happening to Bosnia's multi-ethnic society.

Now, twenty-five years later, here I was discussing the banality of food and restaurants with a resident of that city. He told me about the spectacular wines coming out of the vineyards around Mostar which made it into 'a Balkan version of *Sideways*'. He described how a cousin of his had, against all advice, opened a vegetarian cafe serving paleo cakes. 'In spite of my expecting he wouldn't last longer than half a year tops, the place turned into a big success,' Mirko said. Recently a Spanish couple arrived and opened a tapas bar. It was thriving.

Anybody who has followed Balkan politics will know that the wounds run deep; that the shooting war might be history but that many seriously caustic political and inter-ethnic differences remain. And yet it was clear to me from my discussion with Mirko that food culture had become a way to navigate through some of that. 'The key to happiness here,' he wrote, 'is to pretend you live in a normal society.' What could be more normal than a spot of tapas?

It was not the first time I had experienced this. For the past few years I have been coming and going from Northern Ireland. Each time, I have been struck by the intense interest in food culture among the generation that came to adulthood after the Good Friday Agreement. They also crave a stable form of normality. Saul McConnell is the general manager of Noble, a relatively new bistro just outside Belfast which has rightly won a bunch of awards. He is a part of that generation. As he said to me, 'The hospitality business is a great way to mix and mingle and when you do that everything else is forgotten. We can talk about food rather than all the other things.'

I am a granite-hearted, steely Englishman. I am repulsed when I hear people talk about food 'being cooked with love'. My instinct is to roll my eyes and shout: 'I don't want your bloody love. I want your good taste and skill.' I still hold this to be so. But there is no doubt in my mind that certain of the clichés we trot out about food and community – about the value of sitting down to break bread with each other – are literally true. All too often people who moan about a shoddy restaurant meal or substandard ingredients are dismissed as wallowing in 'first world problems'. It's a crass response. All any of us wants to do is be able to get on with our lives unthreatened by war or calamity. We want to be so safe that we can sweat the small stuff. When we criticise our lunch that's what we are actually talking about: the fact that, happily, life is precisely as it should be.

Patience Is Not a Virtue

In the business of dinner, patience is not a virtue. Patience is proof only of a distinct lack of interest, and where eating is concerned that can never be a good thing. It displays itself most readily at a very middle-class type of dinner party, the sort almost nobody invites me to these days. Just because I'm a restaurant critic they assume I will be rude about their cooking. I always protest. I always say that what really matters to me is the conversation, the people and the banter. This, of course, is a lie; I am incapable of switching off.

But if it means I escape the sort of dinner party where you turn up and are ushered into the living room, only to find the cook sitting there, knocking back the prosecco like a toddler on the Calpol, then that's fine with me. At first, it's okay. There are introductions. There are nibbles. There is chat. And then a second bottle is opened and still the cook doesn't leave us. Now my anxiety levels rise. Surely, at some point they'll want to go and do something with food. I know I would. But no. The glass is emptied. A third bottle is opened. Somebody says something that reveals them to be an unreconstructed bigot. Now I am drunk. And hungry. As the Hulk never said, don't make me hungry; you wouldn't like me when I'm hungry.

Eventually, of course, the cook saunters off to the kitchen, but by then I already know the pickings will be dismal. Because nobody with a real instinct to feed, which means someone who cooks out of their own greed as much as everybody else's, would have been popping the corks in the living room. They would have been by the stove, cooing over their bubbling pots, wet-lipped with eagerness. In these circumstances patience is never its own reward. It is a punishment for some nameless crime.

The curious thing is that I actually have no problem waiting for food, as long as I know how long I have to wait. One recent Sunday, for example, I got up and, while still in my dressing gown, seasoned and seared two joints of pork. I fried some lardons with a mirepoix, then deglazed the pan with white wine and stock. All that took about an hour. I returned the meat to the pan and let it braise for another five hours on a low heat. I removed the meat and let it cool for an hour or two, while reducing the liquor by a third. I cut the pork into inch-thick slices, and seared them in hot salty butter so the edges were crisp. Finally, I returned them to the pot, alongside a lot of cannellini beans. A few sprigs of fresh thyme, and a mere eight hours after I had begun, our dinner was ready. It was worth the wait.

The point is that I had always known it would take eight hours, had calculated it all into my day; I also knew that there would be important but distracting things along the way, like breakfast and lunch. By contrast, waiting just twenty minutes longer than could ever be considered reasonable in a Devon pub recently left me furious and evil. So what if they make their own terrific pork pies? So what if they make their own marvellous charcuterie, and their own glorious sausages and their own fabulous bacon, from fat and happy pigs? Being forced to wait too long for any of it left me with a nasty taste in the mouth. And that's no way to start lunch.

I Want to Be Alone

According to the Office of National Statistics, there are nearly three million single-occupier households in Britain. Roughly twice as many of us live in solitude now as did in the 1970s. Obviously this has its downsides: morbid self-obsession; a failure to notice you have developed the social habits of a troglodyte, only with fewer language skills; the likelihood that, by living alone, you shall also die alone, your decomposing corpse providing a last festering meal for the nine smelly cats you acquired to keep you company.

But hey, there is a big upside: you have the sublime pleasure of only needing to cook for yourself. Don't get me wrong. I like cooking for other people (and if any of my family is reading this, really darlings, nothing gives me more joy than keeping you fed). But cooking only for yourself, well now, that's the real deal. I am always baffled when anyone announces they don't bother bashing the pans about if they are the only person who needs to eat. My conclusion is: they're not proper greedy enough. Cook for others and, however appreciative, there will always be something they don't like. They will turn their nose up at that brilliant thing you do with butternut squash, thyme and bacon. Or the excellent braised peas you make with cos lettuce. And bacon. Or the squidgy brownie with 70 per cent cocoa solids and pecans. And bacon.

Cooking for yourself is cooking for someone you love. It's a night in with your favourite person. It is a culinary event without compromise. It is a very special kind of self-pleasure. An example. I love baking sausages on a bed of sliced onions and mushrooms. And bacon. A dribble of olive oil, a splash of balsamic vinegar, a good heat, and let everything caramelise. The fat from the sausages runs into the onions. The vinegar cooks down to a sweet-savoury sticky syrup. There are crisp bits and salty bits and sweet bits. Now, normally if I am cooking this for a bunch of people I have to stop when the onions have gone golden brown. Which is fine.

But fine is boring. Fine is polite, and when I'm alone, politeness can go hang. For there's another stage beyond golden brown when the balsamic turns the onions black and crunchy. It's a kind of controlled burning. It is, I accept, an acquired taste, but it is one I have fully acquired. And so, when I am cooking for myself, when nobody else is there to pull a face or shout 'How could you?' or 'I thought you were meant to have refined tastes but it turns out you have the palate of an agricultural worker who lost their tongue to a threshing machine,' I can brutalise those onions to my heart's content. I can spank them until they're begging for mercy. I can show them who's boss. Oh joy.

If I'm only cooking for myself, I can get my butcher to cut my steak a good three inches thick, while others I cook for would regard that as just too much cow (explain too much?). I can bash salted anchovies into the butter, without worrying about children shouting 'too fishy!' I can turn the chilli heat in my Thai green curry to ten, put flakes of sea salt on my chocolate ice cream with impunity. In short I can do what the hell I like. And frankly that's worth a little loneliness. I may not have Greta Garbo's looks. I definitely don't have her figure. But when it comes to dinner I, like the smouldering Swede, also want to be alone.

Farewell Hugh

Every week I receive emails requesting specific restaurant recommendations. There are significant birthdays that need marking, cantankerous relatives that need placating. I try but don't always manage to answer them all. The one I received at the end of May demanded an answer. Hugh Paton wanted my top ten places in the UK; not gastro palaces offering experiences that would stay with him for the rest of his life, because it turned out there wasn't much of that life left. He had recently been given a terminal cancer diagnosis, and was no longer in the business of creating memories. As he put it, 'Going and eating a few decent meals strikes me as one good way to spend some of my remaining time.'

I wrote him a list: the ramshackle Company Shed for bare-bones seafood on the Essex coast; the vivid, live-fire cooking of Träkol on the Gateshead side of the Tyne; the Game Bird at the Stafford hotel in London for a bit of old-school British classicism, and so on. Because people like lists, I posted it to Twitter, explaining the context. The response was immense. People tweeted the restaurants they would go to in the same circumstances. They discussed the pleasures of a good meal in bad times. They celebrated the dishes that would most give them comfort.

Touchingly, many of the restaurants then stepped up, offering Hugh and his other half lunch on them. Emails flew back and forth. Introductions were made. At one point he emailed his thanks but said he might leave it a month or two until treatment was underway. I counselled him against that. I had recently lost one of my closest friends to a similar cancer and knew full well that while you hope for time, it's not a commodity you can bank on. 'Carpe diem and all that,' I said.

He took my advice. 'OK,' he wrote back. 'Carpe diem it is.' There were, by all accounts, wonderful meals at Margot and Rochelle Canteen at the ICA in London, and a trip to Parker's Tavern in Cambridge, where a fire alarm forced them all out on to the street. Hugh was given a doorman's plum-coloured coat against the chill, and was photographed in it, drink still in hand. He was the recipient of the kindness of strangers. But those three restaurants were all he managed. Hugh died towards the end of July, just two months after he first emailed me.

Although we never met, other than via email, I came to like Hugh very much; I admired his phlegmatic approach to the hand that life had dealt him. I especially appreciated his approach to restaurants. As far as he was concerned, they weren't providing meals to be captured and pinned to a board like so many butterflies, stiffened with rigor mortis. They were about life, lived firmly in the present tense.

We are all of us prone to dwell on the future: on that job or relationship which will finally gift us the happiness we so crave. But if you can afford it, a good meal, in a restaurant engineered to feed rather than impress, forces us into the now. And the now was exactly where Hugh needed to be. As his partner Anna put it to me, after Hugh had died, 'For the last time he could enjoy the taste, the ambience and the people who treated us with touching consideration.' It's easy to dismiss a meal out as just lunch. It's easy to see it as ephemeral. But sometimes, just sometimes, it can be so very much more.

In memory of Hugh Paton, 1952–2019.

Acknowledgements

The quotation from the historian Rachel Laudan, in the column entitled 'Due Process' (page 19), comes from an interview with Laudan by the writer and historian Maureen Ogle from 2013. All the columns in this book appeared first in *Observer Food Monthly* between March 2010 and February 2020. I am therefore indebted to Allan Jenkins and Gareth Grundy, editor and deputy editor respectively of *OFM*, who gave me the fabulous soapbox of a column, let me write about what I felt was most pressing and from time to time saved me from myself when my attempts at jokes had wandered too far off-piste. I should also like to record my gratitude to the three editors of the *Observer* that I have worked for: Roger Alton, John Mulholland and, latterly, Paul Webster. Without their patronage I wouldn't have been able to have the gig in the first place. I am grateful to Guardian News and Media Limited for granting me the rights to republish these columns in this collection. My original editor at Faber, Fred Baty, brought this project to life and Ruth O'Loughlin shepherded it into the world. The entire team at Faber have been a joy to work with. Thanks, too, to my agent Jonny Geller and his colleagues at Curtis Brown.

Finally, I must thank my family: my wife Pat and my sons Eddie and Dan, who have regularly had to put up with me at the dinner table, trying out one argument or another to see if it would fly as a column. They laughed in all the right places. Sometimes.

Also by Jay Rayner

Wasted Calories and Ruined Nights: A Journey Deeper into Dining Hell

Jay Rayner isn't just a trifle irritated. He is eye-gougingly, bone-crunchingly, teeth-grindingly angry. And admit it, that's why you picked up this book, isn't it?

Because you aren't really interested in glorious prose poems celebrating the finest dining experience known to humanity, are you? You want him to suffer abysmal cooking, preferably at eye-watering prices, so you can gorge on the details and luxuriate in vicarious displeasure. You're in luck. Revel in Jay's misfortune as he is subjected to dreadful meat cookery with animals that died in vain, gravies full of casual violence and service that redefines the word 'incompetent'.

He hopes you enjoy reading his reviews of these twenty miserable meals a damn sight more than he didn't enjoy experiencing them.